Statistical Analysis Handbook
Minitab® Version 21
by George Lee Sye

SOARENT PUBLISHING

PO Box 267, Ravenshoe, Qld, AUSTRALIA, 4888

www.georgeleesye.com/books

© 2023 by Soarent Publishing (George Lee Sye) - All Rights Reserved

Software Version

3rd Update for Minitab® Version 21

Minitab software s is available for a 30-day FREE trial directly from - www.Minitab.com

Six Sigma is a registered trademark of Motorola Inc.

Minitab® is a registered trademark of Minitab Inc.

(Print Version) ISBN 978-0-9870850-1-6

MINITAB STATISTICAL ANALYSIS HANDBOOK - VERSION 21

TABLE OF CONTENTS

1. Common Functions 13

    1.01 Importing Excel Files   13

    1.02 Changing Data Types (Text and Numeric Data)   14

    1.03 Stacking Columns   15

    1.04 Unstacking Columns   16

    1.05 Merging Worksheets   17

    1.06 Sorting Columns   18

    1.07 Column Statistics   19

    1.08 Minitab Shortcuts   20

2. Understanding and Using P-Values 21

    2.01 P-Values Overview   21

    2.02 Summary of P Values and Hypothesis   22

3. Descriptive Statistics 23

    3.01 Descriptive Stats Summary with Histogram   23

4. Displaying Frequency Distributions 25

    4.01 Frequency Distributions for Categorical Data   25

    4.02 Pie Chart with Minitab   25

    4.03 Pareto Charts with Minitab   26

    4.04 Frequency Distributions for Numerical Data   27

    4.05 Basic Histogram with Minitab   29

4.06 Simple Boxplot with Minitab - Single Y   30

5. Measurement System Analysis 31

    5.01 What is Measurement System Analysis   31

    5.02 Overview of Gage R&R   31

    5.03 Creating the Gage R&R Study Worksheet   32

    5.04 Gage R&R with Minitab (Crossed)   34

    5.05 Interpreting Results   35

6. Process Capability 36

    6.01 Process Capability Overview   36

    6.02 Undertaking Basic Capability Analysis   36

    6.03 Long Term Capability Indices - Pp / Ppk (Normal Data)   39

    6.04 Potential (Short Term) Capability Indices - Cp and Cpk   39

    6.05 Capability Analysis Six Pack   40

7. Normality of Data 41

    7.01 What is Normality Testing?   41

    7.02 Subjective Normality Testing   41

    7.03 Statistical Testing of Normality - Anderson Darling   42

8. Data Transformation 45

    8.01 Overview   45

    8.02 Box Cox Transformation   45

9. Capability Analysis with Transformation 46

    9.01 Capability Analysis (With Transformation)   46

10. Process Stability Analysis 48

    10.01 Run Charts Overview   48

    10.02 Run Charts with Minitab   49

    10.03 Using P Values with Run Chart Non Parametric Tests   50

    10.04 Control Charts Overview   50

    10.05 Setting Minitab Control Chart Defaults   51

    10.06 Choosing The Relevant Control Chart   53

    10.07 Variable Data - I-MR Chart   55

    10.08 Variable Data - Xbar-R Chart   56

    10.09 Variable Data - Xbar-S Chart   57

    10.10 Variable Data - Separating Data Into Stages on the Same Chart   58

    10.11 Variables Data - Zone Chart   60

    10.12 Variables Data - CUSUM Chart   61

    10.13 Adding Reference Lines to Control Charts   63

    10.14 Attribute Data - NP Chart   64

    10.15 Attribute Data - P Chart   64

    10.16 Attribute Data - U Chart   65

    10.17 Attribute Data - C Chart   65

11. Stratifying Data - Sources of Variation 66

    11.01 What is Stratification   66

    11.02 Stratified Pie Charts   67

    11.03 Stratified Histograms   69

11.04 Stratified Boxplots - Single Y 70

11.05 ANOM Chart for Means - Normal Data Only 71

11.06 ANOM Chart for Binomial and Poisson Data 72

11.07 Stratification with Pivot tables / Pivot Charts 73

11.08 Setting Up The Pivot Chart 77

12. Hypothesis Testing Overview 80

12.01 The Hypothesis Testing Process 80

12.02 Choosing Hypothesis Tests – Decision Flowchart 81

12.03 Summary of Hypothesis Testing Tools 82

13. Hypothesis Testing Tools in Detail 83

13.01 Stating Hypothesis Test Conclusions 83

13.02 Chi-Square Test for Association 83

13.03 1 Proportion Test 89

13.04 2 Proportion Test 91

13.05 Test for Equal Variances 93

13.06 1 Sample t-test 98

13.07 1 Sample Sign-test 101

13.08 2 Sample t-test 102

13.09 Mann Whitney Test 104

13.10 Paired t-test 106

13.11 One Way ANOVA 108

13.12 Mood's Median Test 113

14. Hypothesis Testing Application Examples 115

14.01 Hypothesis Testing – General Application 115

14.02 Hypothesis Testing – Six Sigma Projects 117

15. Correlation Analysis 119

15.01 Correlation versus Regression 119

15.02 The Process 119

15.03 Visual Correlation Analysis 119

15.04 Compute Correlation (Includes Matrix Plot) 124

15.05 Summary of Terms – Correlation 127

16. REGRESSION MODELLING 128

16.01 Correlation versus Regression 128

16.02 The Process 128

16.03 Developing a Simple Regression Model 129

16.04 Check Validity Of The Regression Model 132

16.05 Developing a Multiple Linear Regression Model 133

16.06 Check Validity Of The Regression Model 136

16.07 Summary of Terms – Linear Regression 137

17. Two Way ANOVA / Balanced Anova 139

17.01 Experimental Design Process 139

17.02 Two Way ANOVA (Balanced ANOVA) 140

17.03 Main Effects Plot 143

17.04 Interactions Plot 144

18. DESIGN OF EXPERIMENTS (FACTORIAL) 145

    18.01 Experimental Design Process   145

    18.02 Check Orthogonality of the Design   146

    18.03 Designing the Experiment   146

    18.04 Analysing the Experiment   149

    18.05 Reducing the Model   151

    18.06 Changing The Way The Design Is Displayed   154

    18.07 Check Validity of the Model Using Residuals   155

    18.08 Factorial Plots for Designed Experiments   156

    18.09 Response Optimization   158

19. Bibliography 161

20. The Author 162

Foreword

As many of you may have already found out, it's very difficult to make a lot of sense from raw data.

The *most* effective way to analyse data is to *first* present it in such a way that it is informative. This processing of raw data is how we convert it into information. Now while information is not the end point, many organisations find it difficult to move beyond this point.

You look around in large organisations and find that there is a ton of data and information out there. Just take a look inside the hallways of a company that is active in posting this information up for employees to view. There are graphical representations of how processes and employees are performing, the year to date safety results, how much has been spent each month, weekly production rates, and much more. Some of this information is based on the total population of data, however much of it is based on *samples* of data.

Its usefulness can only be realised when the organisation is able to turn this information into *knowledge*, as that is the foundation for taking action. Let me give you a non-work example.

Suppose we collect a sample of data comprising 30 golf scores from one golfer. This is raw data, and in its current form is not useful. The average of these scores is 83. This is information that tells us something about the scores. This is not sufficient however, to give the golfer a foundation for taking action. By studying the data and finding out that there is a direct relationship between the number of putts made and the resulting score, this is now knowledge that allows the golfer to take some action that will impact the scores she is able to achieve.

This wall between information and knowledge is common.

The strength of any effective continual process improvement strategy will lie in its drive towards turning raw data into useful knowledge about the process that can be acted upon. In essence, the focus of such an initiative will be on statistical thinking that takes us beyond the information wall.

Many people fear statistics, and probably for good reason.

Those of you who studied statistics at school or university may have found the subject quite daunting. The equations, the steps required to get to a somewhat unclear destination may have left you feeling drained, and exasperated I might add. Most of us, if not all, spent months studying the formula and equations in order to understand the underlying theory of statistical methods.

There is also the effect of the negative perceptions that many people convey to others when the word 'statistics' is mentioned. When I first asked for advice in regard to the order of subjects to study in obtaining my MBA in the late 90s, it was suggested to me that I do the 'hard one' first ... quantitative analysis or what we refer to as *statistics*.

Many of you may have heard this type of statement yourself. Over time, this constant theme causes us to form negative associations with statistics.

Those associations can and should be changed!

Statistical thinking is *necessary* in any effective process improvement endeavour in any organisation. In fact statistical thinking will be an absolute must for managers of the future, particularly in this world of constant change, vast volumes of data, and the need to differentiate oneself for workplace survival. The ability to make low risk decisions using only samples of data will come to the fore with the growing need to improve faster and compete more effectively.

The question is how do we change those associations?

> *Today, practitioners do not have to study all of the underlying theory to be able to effectively employ statistical methods. We now have the ability to accelerate the learning process and simplify the application of statistics in meaningful ways through the use of statistical analysis software packages such as Minitab.*

The underlying formulas, equations and theory, whilst an important foundation, do not necessarily have to be the focus of the learning process. Application of the tools taught and interpretation of the results is key to moving us quickly to a point where we can add value to the work we do every day in our organisations.

This Handbook

This text has been developed for the purpose of providing business improvement practitioners and line managers with a simple guide to the use of **Minitab Software** in the application of the statistical analysis tools of Six Sigma.

It is designed to accompany specific training journals or other training material that provide all of the relevant information surrounding the tools and processes of Lean Six Sigma.

The text is laid out in such a way that it provides a summary of notations associated with each tool, followed by the menu commands to follow when using Minitab Software.

Referencing Process Mastery with Lean Six Sigma

This handbook can be read in conjunction with my primary Lean Six Sigma publication - **Process Mastery with Lean Six Sigma 2nd Ed**. - the most comprehensive, yet profoundly simple body of knowledge available for Lean and Six Sigma practitioners today.

Click here for more information - https://www.9skillsfactory.com/processmasterywithleansixsigma

Minitab Conventions

Typographical conventions used in this book are consistent with those presented in original text and the Minitab help index.

This how those conventions work.

Convention Example 1

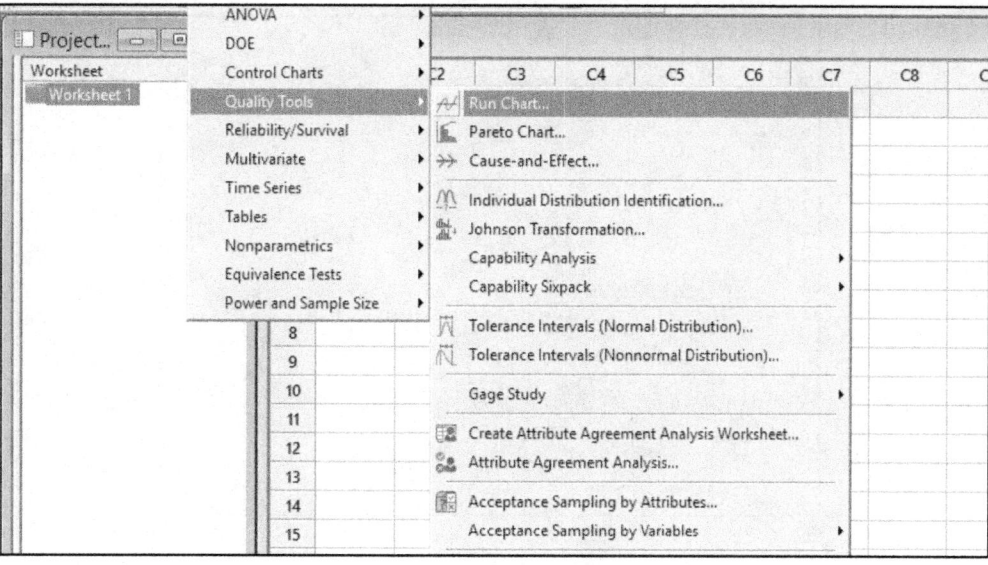

The convention associated with the diagram above is this.

> ❦ Choose **Stat > Quality Tools > Run Chart**

Explanation of Example 1

This notation denotes a menu command. In this case you should choose 'Stat' from the tool menu, then select 'Quality Tools' and 'Run Chart' from the choices offered.

Convention Example 2

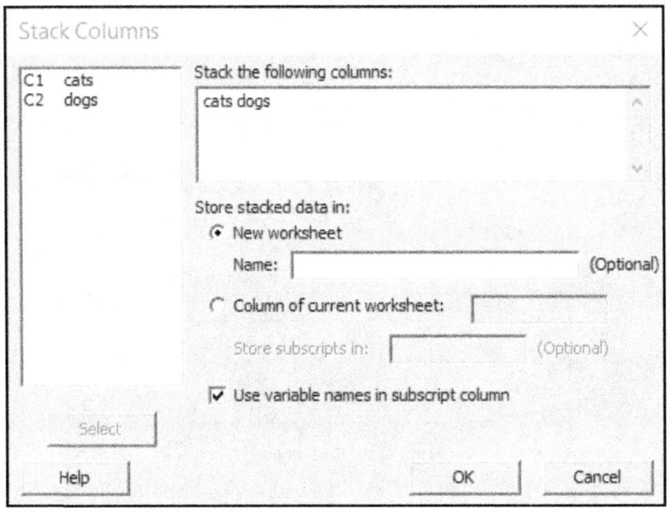

The convention associated with the diagram above is this.

- Choose columns and then Click **Select**
- Click **OK**

Explanation of Example 2

These notations refer to a particular action to take with respect to the dialogue box you are working with.

George Lee Sye - February 2023

'I often say that when you can measure what you are speaking about and express it in numbers, you know something about it, but when you cannot measure it, when you cannot express it in numbers, your knowledge is of a meagre and unsatisfactory kind.'

Lord William Thomson Kelvin

MINITAB STATISTICAL ANALYSIS HANDBOOK - VERSION 21

1. COMMON FUNCTIONS

1.01 Importing Excel Files

Excel worksheets can be imported into Minitab.

1. Choose **File > Open**
2. Select the worksheet and Click **Open**

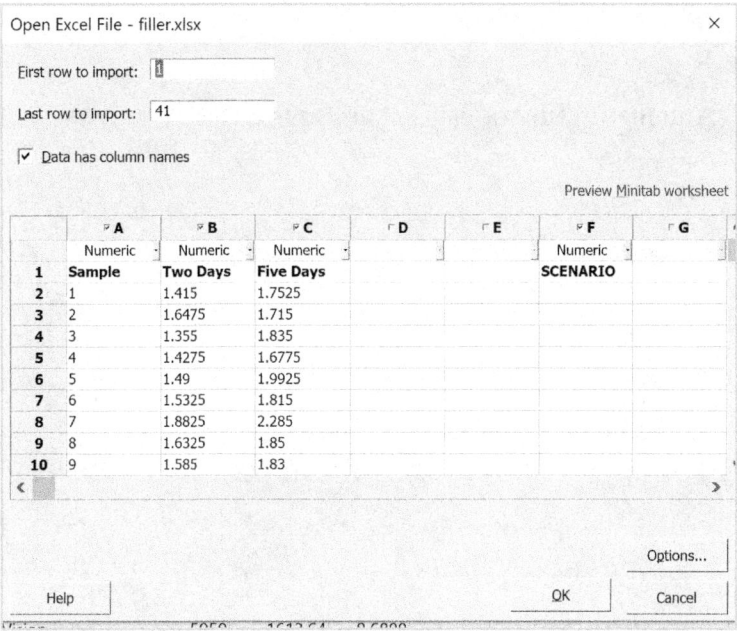

3. Select **Options** (complete as required)
4. Click **OK** in all dialogue boxes

1.02 Changing Data Types (Text and Numeric Data)

Minitab is sensitive to the type of data a column contains. There will be occasions when data is stored in the wrong format, and it will be necessary to convert data (ie: text to numeric and vice versa)

Changing Text to Numeric / Numeric to Text

1. Choose **Data > Change Data Type**
2. Click on **Column Containing Data**
3. Choose **Select**
4. **Choose type:** (Automatic numeric or Text as required)
5. Click **OK**

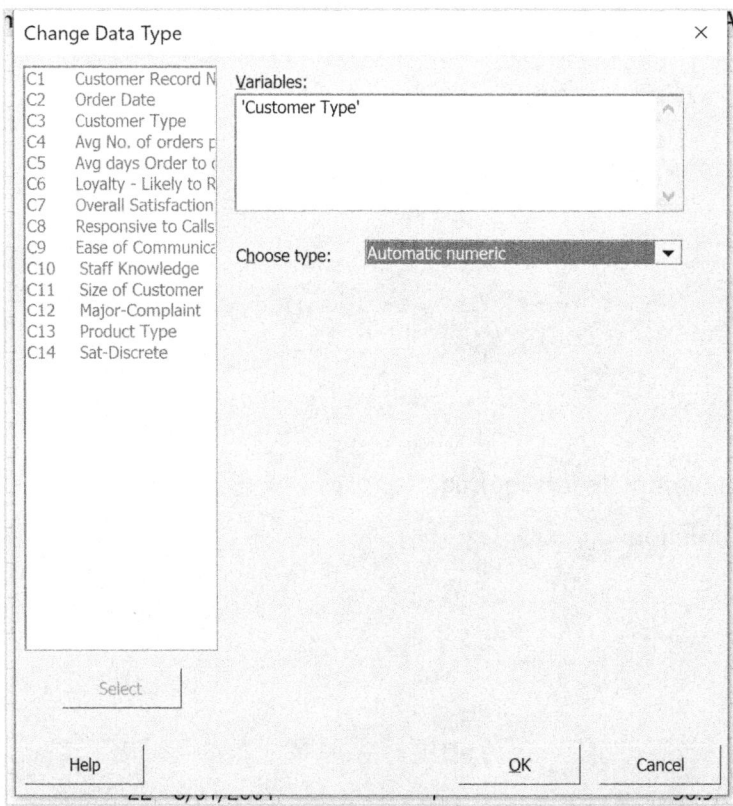

1.03 Stacking Columns

Stacking columns involves the generation of a single column of data (the variable of interest) that is paired to another column containing categorical data (subscripts).

The table to the right shows a set of data stored in unstacked format. To stack these columns …….

1. Choose **Data > Stack > Columns**
2. **Stack the following columns:** (insert columns to be stacked – 'C1' 'C2' 'C3')
3. **Store stacked data in:** (select new worksheet or in current worksheet – subscripts column will contain a reference to the name of each column, paired with each individual variable)
4. Click **OK**

	C1	C2	C3
	A	B	C
1	1.883	1.511	1.427
2	1.715	1.457	1.344
3	1.799	1.548	1.404
4	1.768	1.435	1.548
5	1.711	1.572	1.435
6	1.832	1.486	1.572
7	1.715	1.511	1.548
8	1.799	1.457	1.435

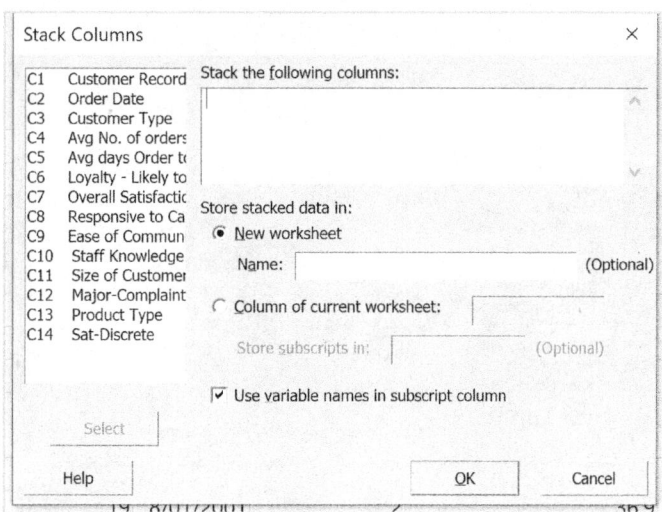

1.04 Unstacking Columns

Unstacking columns involves the generation of a column of data for each group of variables – grouped by relevant subscripts.

The table to the right shows a set of data stored in stacked format. To unstack these columns …….

1. Choose **Data > Unstack Columns**
2. **Unstack the data in:** (insert the column containing the data to be unstacked – 'C2 Result')
3. **Using subscripts in:** (insert the column that identifies the categorical variable that will form the column headings – 'C1 Type')
4. **Store unstacked data in:** (select 'new worksheet' or 'after last column in use' – subscripts will form the title of each column)
5. Click **OK**

	C1 Type	C2 Result
1	A	1.883
2	A	1.715
3	A	1.799
4	B	1.511
5	B	1.457
6	B	1.548
7	C	1.427
8	C	1.344

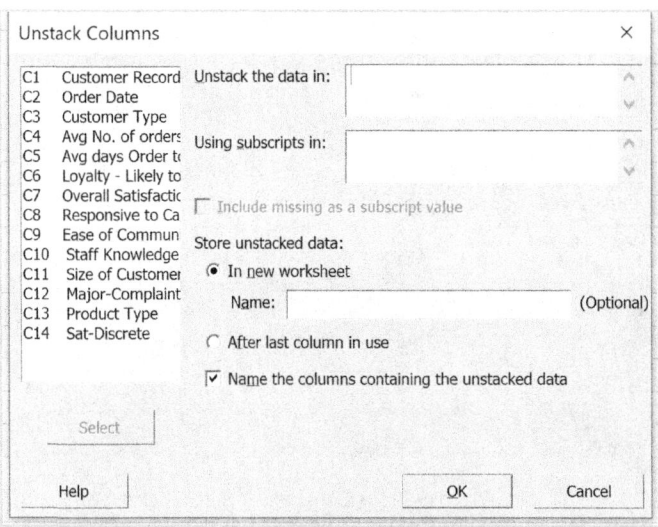

1.05 Merging Worksheets

Used to combine any two open worksheets in a project. This action duplicates and then combines the information from two original worksheets into a new worksheet named Merge Worksheet by default.

1. Make one of the worksheets you want to merge an active window.
2. Choose **Data > Merge Worksheets > Side-by-Side**

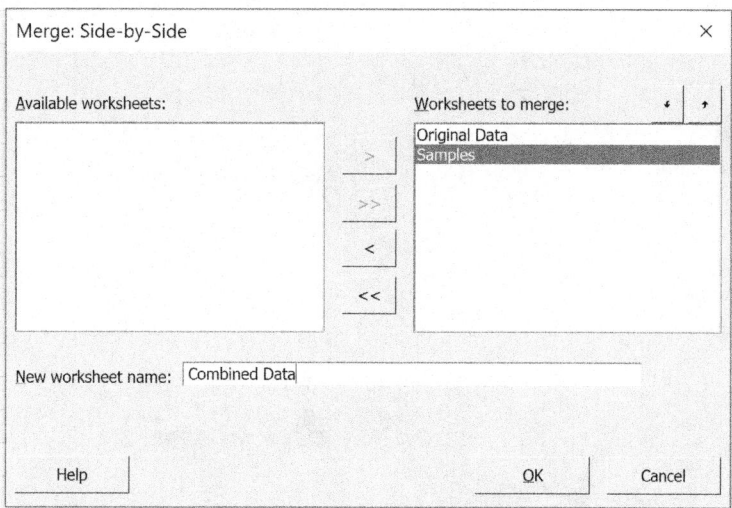

3. **Available worksheets:** (select the worksheets you wish to merge)
4. **New worksheet name:** (enter title of new worksheet)
5. Click **OK**

1.06 Sorting Columns

You can sort one or more columns of data according to values in specifically nominated columns. Sorting simply 'orders' the data by alphabet or numerically along with the nominated columns. You can sort in ascending or descending order, and you can choose to store sorted data in the original columns, other columns you specify, or in a new worksheet.

1. Choose **Data > Sort**

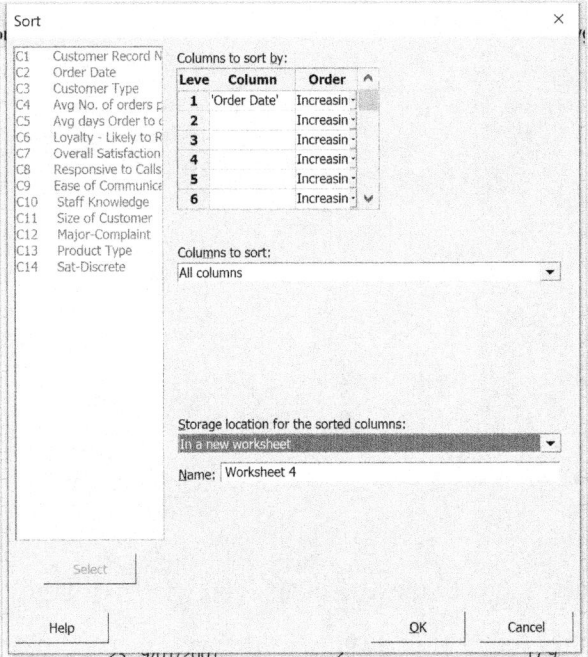

2. **Columns to sort by:** (insert one or more columns to sort)
3. **Order:** (double click to choose increasing or decreasing)
4. **Columns to sort:** (choose all columns or specified columns)
5. **Storage location for the sorted columns:** (choose original columns, end of current worksheet, new worksheet, or end of specified worksheet)
6. Click **OK**

1.07 Column Statistics

Various statistics can be calculated for columns or rows. Column statistics are displayed in the Session window by default, and can be stored as a constant. Row statistics are calculated across the rows of the columns specified and stored in the corresponding rows of a new column.

1. Choose **Calc > Column Statistics**
2. **Statistic:** (select statistics of interest)
3. **Input variable:** (select column to be studied)
4. **Store result in:** (the resulting statistics can be stored in the nominated column)
5. Click **OK** (result will appear in the session window)

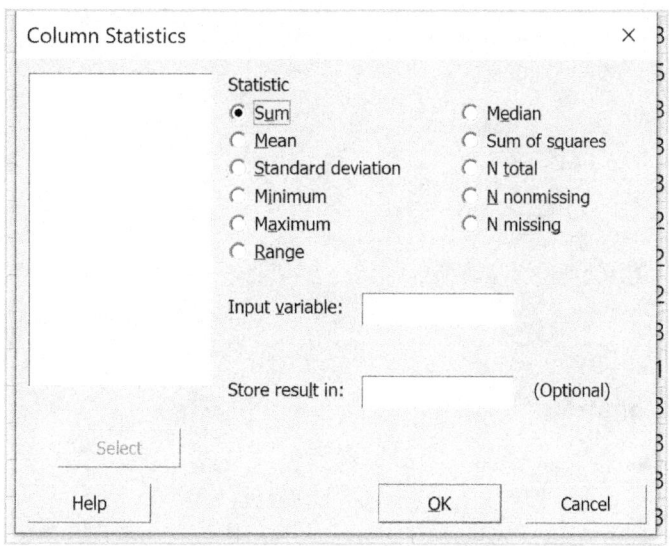

1.08 Minitab Shortcuts

Copy cells or text	Ctrl + C
Cut cells or text	Ctrl + X
Defaults (reset)	F3
Recall Last Dialogue box (edit last)	Ctrl + E
Find cells or text	Ctrl + F
Help	F1
New worksheet or project	Ctrl + N
Open Project	Ctrl + O
Paste cells or text	Ctrl + V
Print Window	Ctrl + P
Project Manager	Ctrl + I
Save Project	Ctrl + S
Select all graphs, cells or text	Ctrl + A
Session Window	Ctrl + M
Shortcut menu (open)	Shift + F10
Stat Guide	Shift + F1
Switch between windows	Ctrl + F6
Worksheet (beginning)	Ctrl + Home
Worksheet (end)	Ctrl + End
Worksheet	Ctrl + D

2. UNDERSTANDING AND USING P-VALUES

2.01 P-Values Overview

Where P values are calculated, they are used in association with some hypothesis.

The Null Hypothesis (HO) is always one that expresses no difference (equal to), and our Alternative Hypothesis (HA) is always one that expresses that there is a difference (less than, greater than or not equal to).

Where a p value is less than the nominated alpha value (α usually = 0.01, 0.05 or 0.10), differences are statistically significant and you reject the null hypothesis that there is no difference. Your conclusion is there is a difference with some risk (α) of being wrong.

P VALUE < ALPHA = <u>REJECT</u> THE NULL HYPOTHESIS

Where a p value is <u>not less than</u> the nominated alpha value, you **do not reject** the null hypothesis and conclude that there is no difference with some degree of confidence (1-α).

This is just a simple explanation of the concept, as any conclusions you write will be more specific.

P VALUE $\geq$ ALPHA = <u>DO NOT REJECT</u> THE NULL HYPOTHESIS

The alpha value, referred to as the level of significance, is an indication of the level of risk you are prepared to accept that if you reject the null hypothesis and conclude that there is a difference, when in fact there is none.

The table on the following page shows the relationship between p values and respective hypotheses for different statistical analysis tools.

2.02 Summary of P Values and Hypothesis

```
                              Alpha (α)
                   ┌──────────────┬──────────────────┐
                   │  Rejection   │  Non Rejection   │
P Values    0.00   ├──────────────┼──────────────────┤  1.00
                   │   Region     │     Region       │
                   └──────────────┴──────────────────┘
```

TOOL	H_A	H_O
Normality Tests	Not from a normal population	Comes from a normal population
1 Sample t Test	μ (< > ≠) (a value)	μ = (a specific value)
1 Sample Sign Test	Median (< > ≠) (a value)	Median = (a specific value)
2 Sample t Test	μ_1 (< > ≠) μ_2	$\mu_1 = \mu_2$
Mann Whitney Test	Median$_1$ (< > =) Median$_2$	Medians are =
Paired t Test	Mean difference (< > ≠) 0	Mean difference = 0
Test for Equal Variances	σ^2's ≠	σ^2's =
1 Way ANOVA	μ's ≠	μ's =
Moods Median Test	Medians ≠	Medians =
Chi Square	Proportions ≠	Proportions are =
2 Way ANOVA	Row factor μ's ≠ Column factor μ's ≠	Row factor μ's are equal Column factor μ's are equal
Full and Fractional Factorial DOE (Effects and Coefficient table)	Effect ≠ 0	Effect = 0
Full and Fractional Factorial DOE (ANOVA)	Effect ≠ 0	Effect = 0
Correlation	Correlation Coef. (R) ≠ 0	Correlation Coef. (R) = 0
Regression	Regression Coef. ≠ 0	Regression Coef. = 0

3. DESCRIPTIVE STATISTICS

Descriptive statistics can be generated for entire data sets or for stratified data sets.

3.01 Descriptive Stats Summary with Histogram

1. Click **Stat > Basic Statistics > Graphical Summary**

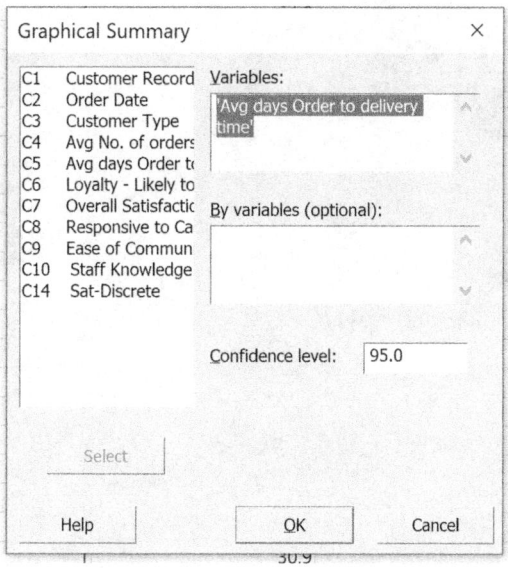

2. Make the **Variables:** cell active
3. Select Column of interest and (this is the variable being studied)
4. Click **Select**
5. Make the **By variables (optional):** cell active if you want to stratify the data
6. Select the column with the stratification variable in it
7. Click **Select**
8. Click **OK**

Minitab produces a descriptive statistics summary that includes histogram and associated statistics as shown in the example.

Graphical Summary

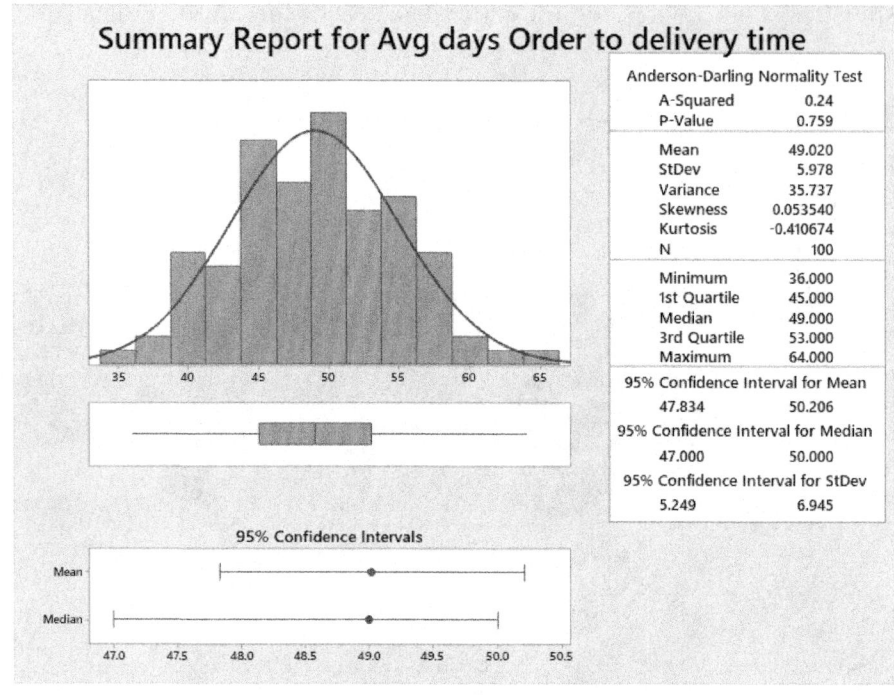

4. DISPLAYING FREQUENCY DISTRIBUTIONS

4.01 Frequency Distributions for Categorical Data

Frequency distributions for categorical data show the categories into which data is partitioned, and the number of units that fall into each category. For example, the number of students enrolled at a college is displayed in the following frequency distribution.

Frequency Distribution for students enrolled at ABC College by classification.

	(Frequency)	(Relative Frequency)
Pre School	248	6.96%
Junior School	1,655	46.42%
Middle School	582	16.33%
Senior School	1,080	30.29%
TOTALS	3,565	100.00%

One of the most expedient ways to convert data into useful information is to represent data in the form of charts. The most common charts used with displaying categorical frequency distributions in MInitab are pie charts and Pareto charts.

4.02 Pie Chart with Minitab

1. Click **Graph > Pie Chart**

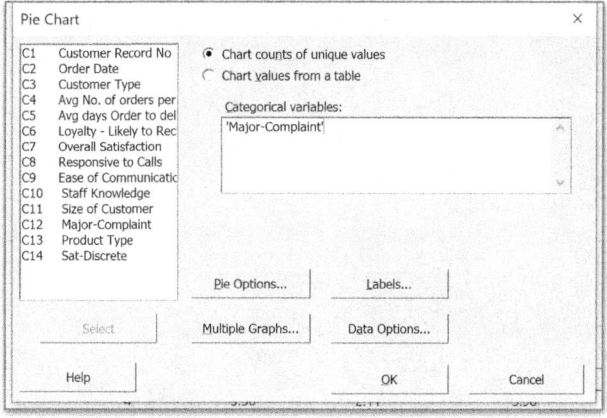

2. Select **'Chart counts of unique values'** (if data you are counting is in a single column)
3. Make the **Categorical variables:** cell active
4. Select and **insert column of interest** (the data you will count)
5. Select Labels
6. Select Slice Labels tab
7. Choose labels you want to display
8. Click **OK** in all dialogue boxes

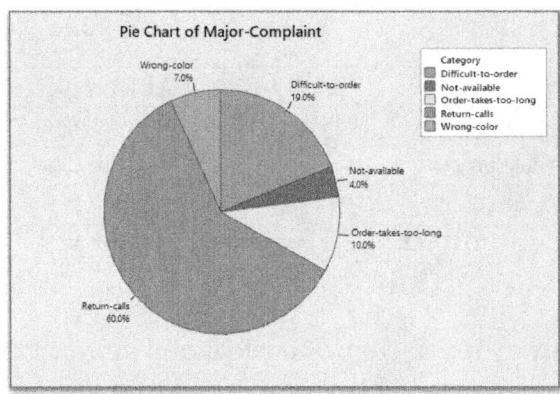

4.03 Pareto Charts with Minitab

1. Click **Stat > Quality Tools > Pareto Chart**
2. Select and insert column containing data you want to count in the **Defects or attribute data in:** cell
3. To stratify charts, insert stratification variable in the **BY variables in:** cell
4. Click **OK**

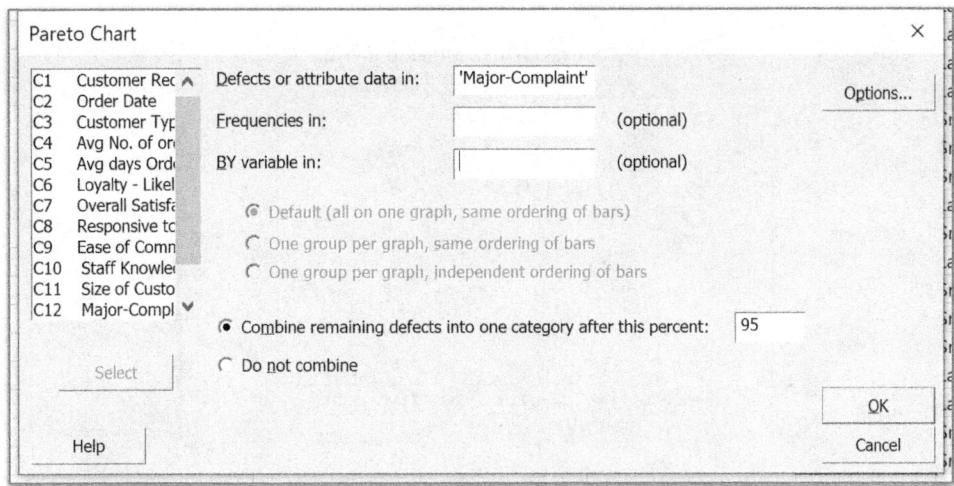

5. Click **OK**

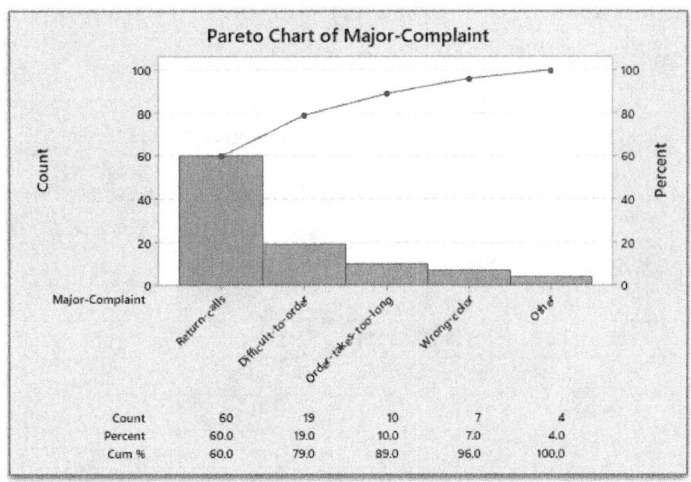

4.04 Frequency Distributions for Numerical Data

Frequency distributions for numerical data show the distribution of data across an ordinal scale. To illustrate the concept, consider the table of data below which shows a sample of times taken to deliver pizza.

Time taken in minutes to deliver pizza for home delivery.

19.5	13.5	12.5	17	20
19	12.5	17	18.5	22.5
15	14	16	20	18
22	17	14	15	18.5
17.5	16.5	21	15.5	17
20	19	17.5	18	14.5
12.5	15	16.5	16	15.5
17	16	15.5	17	16.6

(File: Pizza Delivery Times)

Frequency Distribution Table

These times can be displayed by showing how many of the values are contained in certain intervals across a measurement scale between 12.5 minutes (the minimum time taken) and 22.5 minutes (the maximum time taken).

Frequency Distribution for Pizza Delivery Times

INTERVAL (minutes)	TALLY	FREQUENCY	RELATIVE FREQUENCY (Proportion)
12.50 – 14.17	111111	6	15.0
14.18 – 15.84	1111111	7	17.5
15.85 – 17.50	11111111111111	14	35
17.51 – 19.17	111111	6	15
19.17 – 20.83	1111	4	10
20.83 – 22.50	111	3	7.5
TOTALS		40	100.0%

The frequency column shows us how many of the values exist in a specific interval – 12.5 minutes to 14.17 minutes.

The most common ways of displaying frequency distributions for numerical data are Histograms and Box Plots.

4.05 Basic Histogram with Minitab

Sometimes called 'Frequency Plots', histograms are used widely by Six Sigma practitioners to study the distribution and characteristics of data.

1. Click **Graph > Histogram**
2. Select **'Simple'** (plotting data in a single histogram)
3. Click **OK**
4. Make the **Graph variables:** cell active
5. Select and insert **Column of interest**

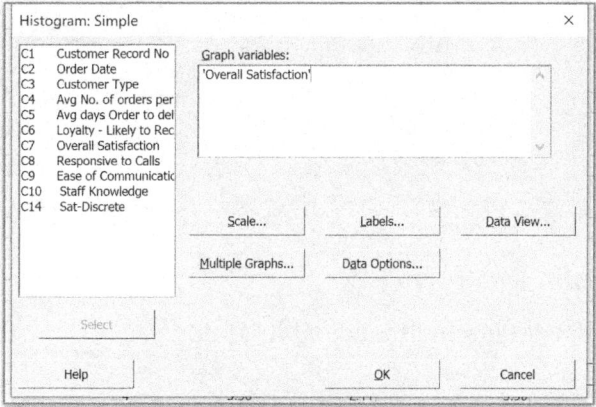

6. Click **OK**

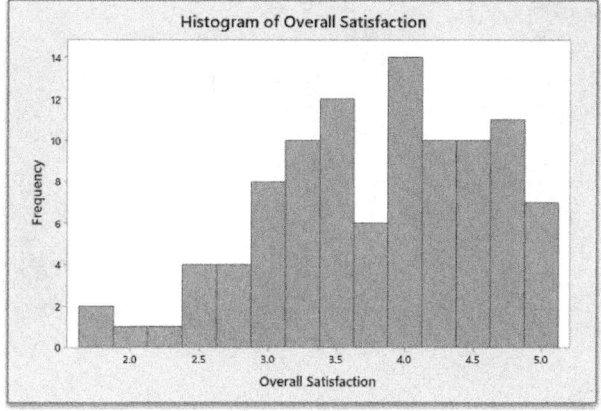

4.06 Simple Boxplot with Minitab - Single Y

1. Click **Graph > Boxplot**
2. Select **'Simple'**
3. Click **OK**

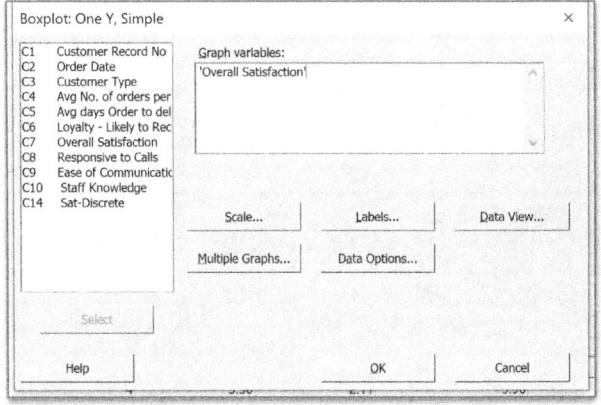

4. Make the **Graph variables:** cell active
5. Select and insert column containing the variable of interest
6. Click **OK**

5. MEASUREMENT SYSTEM ANALYSIS

5.01 What is Measurement System Analysis

The purpose of MSA is ultimately to understand whether or not data collected via a particular measurement system reflects the true variation of the process and does not reflect additional variation introduced by poor measuring. Here we will focus on Gage R&R analysis.

5.02 Overview of Gage R&R

Purpose

The purpose of undertaking Gage R&R is:
- Study the contribution of measurement system error to overall data variation.

Gage R&R does this through analysing:
- The level to which one operator can repeat measurements; and
- The level to which a second operator can reproduce the same results.

Terms

- Crossed – When all operators measure parts from the same batch.
- Nested – When all operators measure different parts such as with destructive testing.
- Attribute - An attribute Gage Study is conducted when measurers make a call about pass or fail of a part rather than undertake some measurement.

Tips for Practitioners

- Plan the study.
- Define the number of parts that span the range of long term variation (typically 10 units).
- Layout the worksheet as shown in the example below.

	C1-T	C2	C3
	PART	Operator	Measure
1	C073	1	14
2	C074	1	17
3	C075	1	16
4	C076	1	14
5	C077	1	13
6	C073	2	14
7	C074	2	14
8	C075	2	16
9	C076	2	16
10	C077	2	17

5.03 Creating the Gage R&R Study Worksheet

1. Choose **Stat > Quality Tools > Gage Study > Create Gage R&R Study Worksheet**

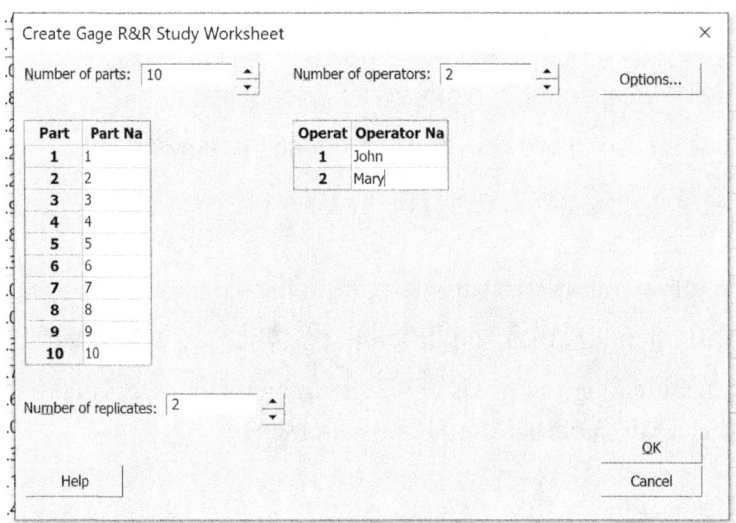

2. **Number of parts:** (insert the number, it defaults to the usual number of 10)
3. **Part name** (insert names if you need to identify parts)
4. **Number of operators:** (minimum of 2)
5. **Operator name** (insert names of all operators)
6. **Number of replicates:** (minimum of 2)
7. Click **OK**

The resulting worksheet is perfectly formatted to run the MSA and capture data for analysis. Notice it is generated with a random run order.

	C1	C2-T	C3-T	C4
	RunOrder	Parts	Operators	
1	1	7	John	
2	2	2	John	
3	3	6	John	
4	4	1	John	
5	5	8	John	
6	6	3	John	
7	7	4	John	
8	8	9	John	
9	9	10	John	
10	10	5	John	
11	11	5	Mary	
12	12	8	Mary	
13	13	7	Mary	
14	14	10	Mary	
15	15	9	Mary	

5.04 Gage R&R with Minitab (Crossed)

1. Choose **Stat > Quality Tools > Gage Study > Gage R&R Study (Crossed)**

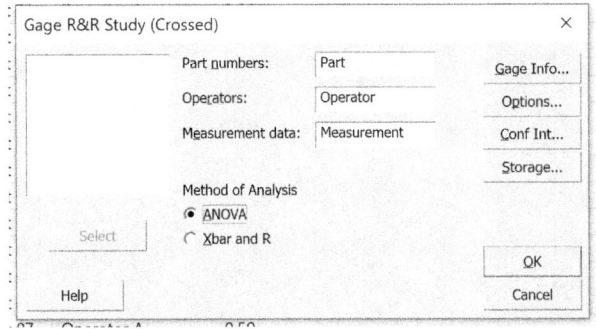

2. **Part Numbers:** (insert column of part names or numbers)
3. **Operators:** (insert column containing the operator names)
4. **Measurement Data:** (insert column of measurement results)
5. Click **OK**

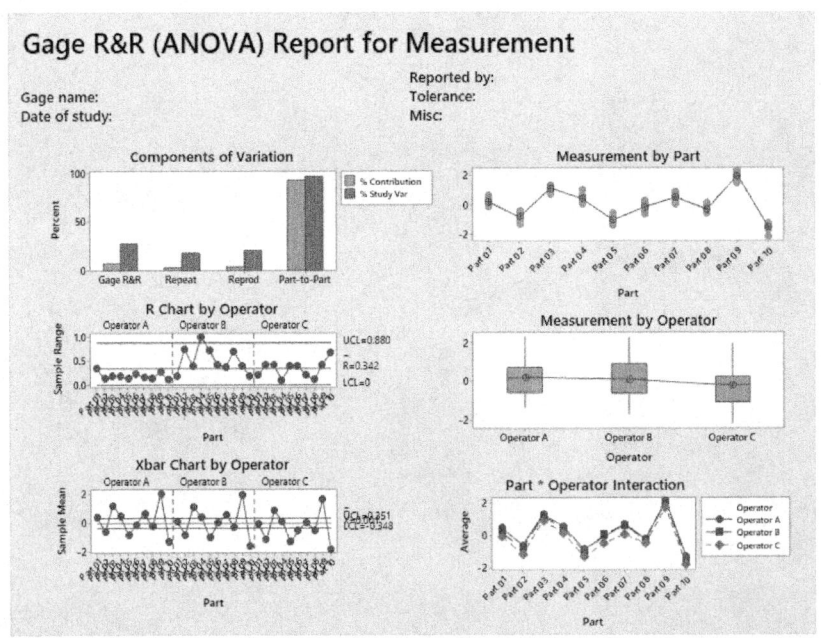

5.05 Interpreting Results

```
AIAG.MTW
Gage R&R Study - ANOVA Method

Total            89    94.6471

Gage R&R

Variance Components
                                %Contribution
Source              VarComp     (of VarComp)
Total Gage R&R      0.09143         7.76
  Repeatability     0.03997         3.39
  Reproducibility   0.05146         4.37
    Operator        0.05146         4.37
Part-To-Part        1.08645        92.24
Total Variation     1.17788       100.00

Gage Evaluation
                                Study Var    %Study Var
Source              StdDev (SD)  (6 × SD)      (%SV)
Total Gage R&R      0.30237      1.81423       27.86
  Repeatability     0.19993      1.19960       18.42
  Reproducibility   0.22684      1.36103       20.90
    Operator        0.22684      1.36103       20.90
Part-To-Part        1.04233      6.25396       96.04
Total Variation     1.08530      6.51180      100.00

Number of Distinct Categories = 4
```

% Contribution (of VarComp) – percent contribution to the overall variation made by each component.

% Study Var – percent of the study variation for each component (these do not add up to 100), sometimes referred to as % P/TV (Precision to Total Variation).

Good and bad values for these results are shown in the following table:

Result	% Contribution	% Study Var (%SV)
Marginal	< 9%	< 30%
Good	< 4%	< 20%
Excellent	< 1%	< 10%

6. PROCESS CAPABILITY

6.01 Process Capability Overview

Terminology

Process capability - The ability of a process to consistently produce a product or service that meets or exceeds customer specifications.

Target value – The ideal value of a characteristic of the process output.

Upper specification limit – Any value above this exceeds customer specification or tolerance.

Lower specification limit – Any value below this is less than customer specification or tolerance.

Capable process – A process where control limits (+/- 3σ) are equal to or within specification limits.

Purpose

- To provide simple method of assessing process capability
- To provide a basis for comparing processes
- To provide a basis for assessing improvement

6.02 Undertaking Basic Capability Analysis

1. Choose **Stat > Quality Tools > Capability Analysis > Normal**
2. **Data arranged as:** (choose *single column* or *subgroups across rows of*)
3. **Single column:** (insert column and subgroup size)

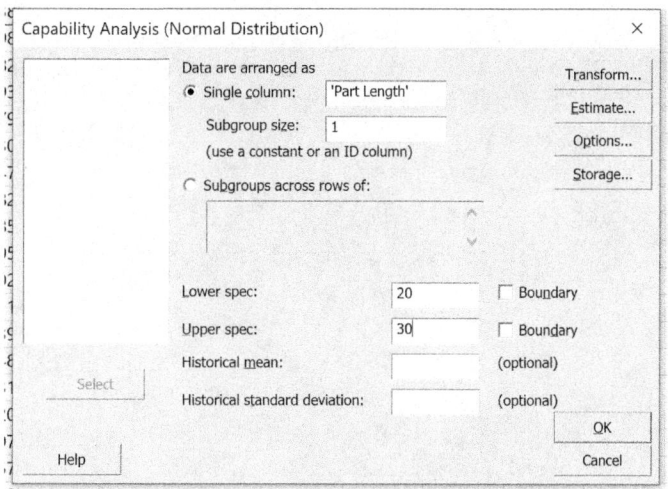

OR ALTERNATIVELY

4. **Subgroups across rows of:** (insert relevant columns)
5. **Lower spec:** (insert customers' LSL)
6. **Upper spec:** (insert customers' USL)
7. Choose **Options**
8. **Target (adds CPM to table):** (insert target value – usually center point between customer specification limits)
9. Click **OK**
10. Choose **Estimate:** (select depending on subgroup size)
11. Click **OK** in all dialogue boxes

MINITAB STATISTICAL ANALYSIS HANDBOOK - VERSION 21

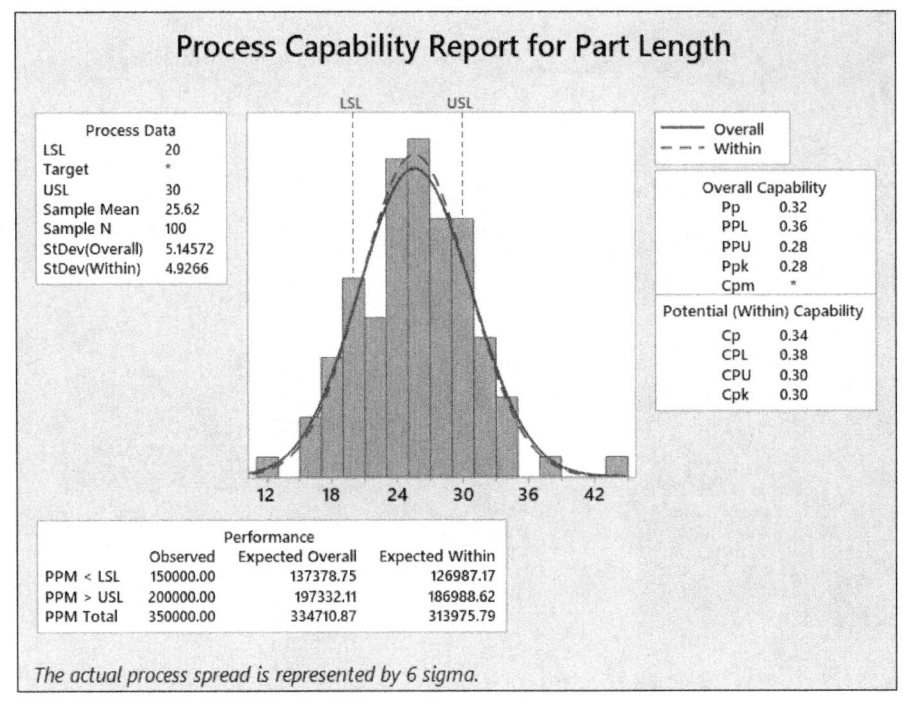

6.03 Long Term Capability Indices - Pp / Ppk (Normal Data)

Pp, Ppk, PPU and PPL represent the *overall capability* of the process, and depicts how the process is actually performing in the long term.

Where Cp and Cpk use an estimated standard deviation and provide an indication of potential capability, Pp and Ppk use actual standard deviation of the data being analysed (assuming it is population standard deviation) and provides an indication of actual capability of the data being analysed.

Note:

- The process must be in a state of statistical control (i.e. a stable process).
- Long Term Capability Indices can only be used when you are working with **data that is normally distributed** for the following reason – 'You will be working with standard deviation, and the proportion of data between + and – 3 standard deviation limits (or control limits) is assumed to be consistent with the properties of a normal distribution'.

6.04 Potential (Short Term) Capability Indices - Cp and Cpk

Potential capability indices utilise a bias correction factor in the equations to estimate population standard deviation and provide an indication of potential capability.

- Cp – The potential capability of the process in the short term (if there were no shift and drift in the process).
- CPU – The short-term ratio of the distance between the upper specification limit and the mean, to three standard deviations.
- CPL - The short-term ratio of the distance between the lower specification limit and the mean, to three standard deviations.
- Cpk – The minimum of either CPU or CPL. (Values => 1 indicate that in the short term, the process is capable)

Cp, Cpk, CPU and CPL represent the potential long-term capability of the process, and depicts how the process would perform in the absence of shifts and drifts in sample means.

Note: Potential Capability Indices can be used with **normal** and **non normal data** as the same bias correction factors used in control chart construction are applied.

6.05 Capability Analysis Six Pack

1. Choose **Stat > Quality Tools > Capability Six Pack > Normal**

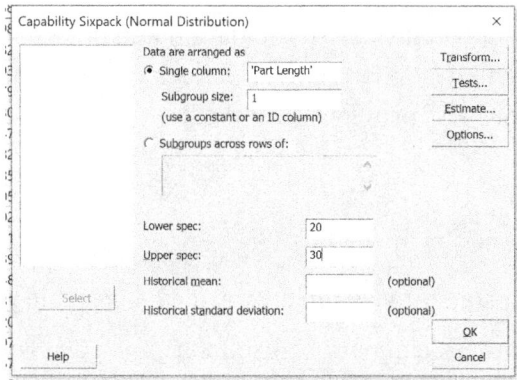

2. **Data arranged as:** (choose *single column* or *subgroups across rows of*)
3. **Single column:** (insert column and subgroup size which is usually 1)
4. Enter **Lower spec:** according to customer requirements (if there is one)
5. Enter **Upper spec:** according to customer requirements (if there is one)
6. Click **OK**

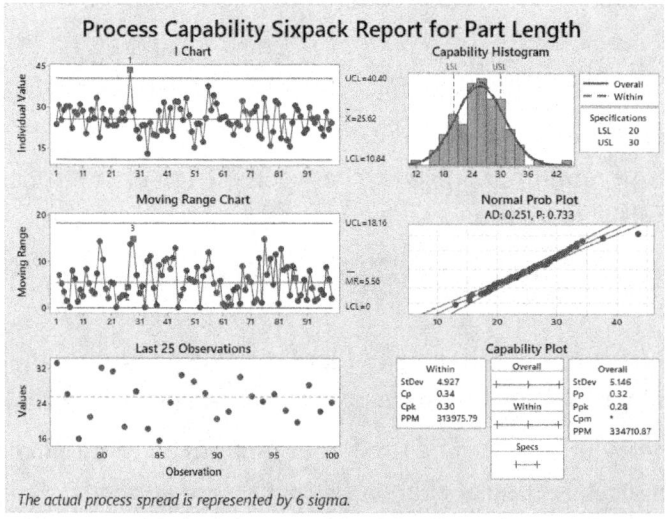

7. NORMALITY OF DATA

7.01 What is Normality Testing?

The purpose of normality testing is to make a determination as to whether or not the data under analysis has the characteristics of a normal distribution.

7.02 Subjective Normality Testing

Histograms

1. Choose **Graph > Histogram**
2. Select type of output from the gallery of graphs (simple, with fit etc)
3. **Graph Variables** (insert column of interest)

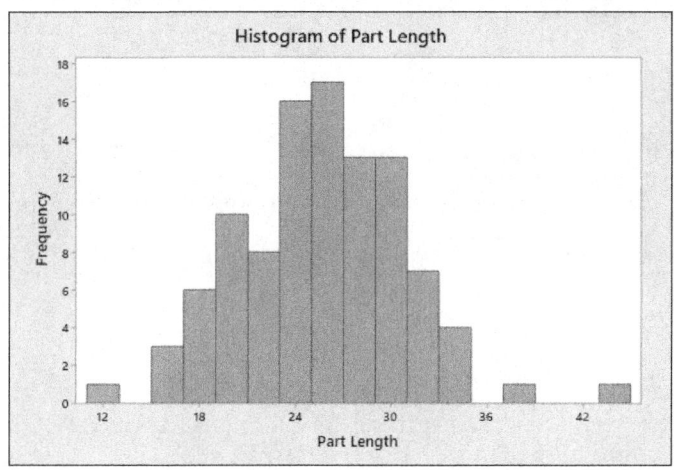

The distribution should reflect the bell shape and symmetry of a normal distribution.

Probability Plots

1. Choose **Graph > Probability Plot**
2. Select **Single** or **Multiple** as required
3. **Graph Variables** (insert column of interest)

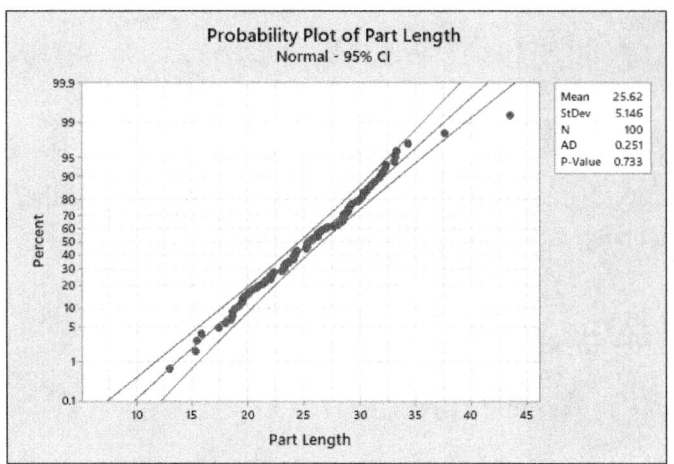

Data should be within confidence interval for normal data and closely fit the straight line.

7.03 Statistical Testing of Normality - Anderson Darling

Normality Testing - Your Null and Alternative Hypothesis

When using p values, the Null and Alternative Hypothesis for normality testing is:

> H_0: Data set *does* come from a Normal Distribution
> H_A: Data set *does not* come from a Normal Distribution

Normality Test

1. Choose **Stat > Basic Statistics > Normality Test**
2. **Variable:** (insert column of interest)
3. **Test for Normality:** (select Anderson-Darling)

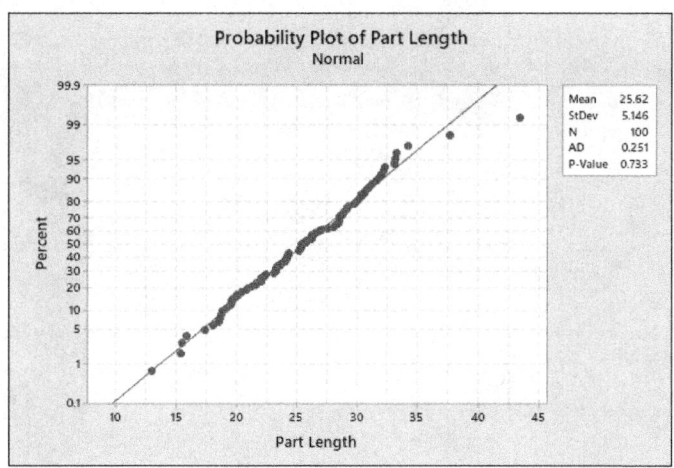

For normal data, the 'p' value is > alpha. the easiest way to remember is this:
- Lo P Value (< 0.05) = Lo Fit with Normal Curve
- Hi P Value (>= 0.05) = Hi Fit with Normal Curve

Descriptive Statistics

1. Choose **Stat > Basic Statistics > Graphical Summary**
2. **Variables:** (insert columns of interest – will create multiple charts)
3. **By variables:** (insert column for stratifying data)
4. **Confidence level:** (default setting is 95 percent)

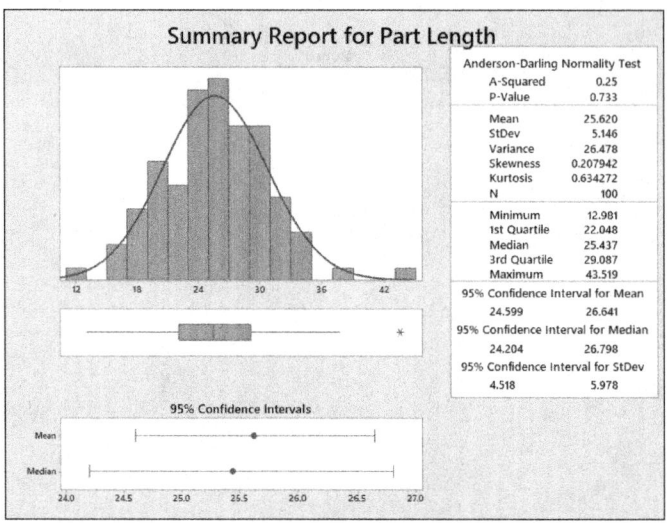

For normal data, the 'p' value is > alpha. the easiest way to remember is this:

- Lo P Value (< 0.05) = Lo Fit with Normal Curve
- Hi P Value (>= 0.05) = Hi Fit with Normal Curve

8. DATA TRANSFORMATION

8.01 Overview

Transformations can be used for – (1) Regression Models, and (2) Capability Analysis
Before transforming, you should test for normality.

8.02 Box Cox Transformation

1. Choose **Stat > Control Charts > Box-Cox Transformation**
2. Choose **All observations for a chart are in one column** (one column of data) OR **All observations for a subgroup are in one row of columns**
3. Insert column or columns of data as required
4. **Subgroup Size:** (insert numeric subgroup size or column that identifies subgroups) NOTE: This choice does not appear when observations for a subgroup are in one row of columns.
5. Choose **Options**
6. **Store transformed data in:** (insert a column reference for storing data)
7. Click **OK** in all dialogue boxes

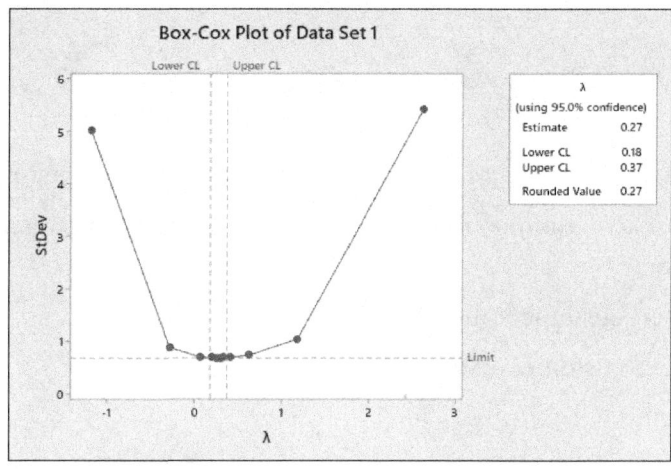

If the confidence interval contains 1, you will not transform the data.

9. CAPABILITY ANALYSIS WITH TRANSFORMATION

Capability analysis with transformation can be undertaken when:

- Data set will transform (and fit the normal distribution); and
- Customer specification limits are transformed at the same time using the same 'transformation'

9.01 Capability Analysis (With Transformation)

1. Choose **Stat > Quality Tools > Capability Analysis > Normal**

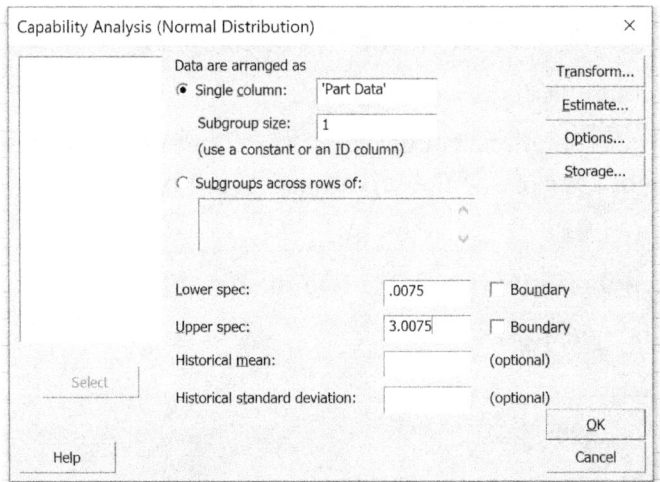

2. **Data arranged as:** (choose *single column* or *subgroups across rows of*)
3. **Single column:** (insert column and subgroup size) OR **Subgroups across rows of:** (insert relevant columns)
4. **Lower spec:** (insert customers' LSL)
5. **Upper spec:** (insert customers' USL)
6. Choose **Transform**

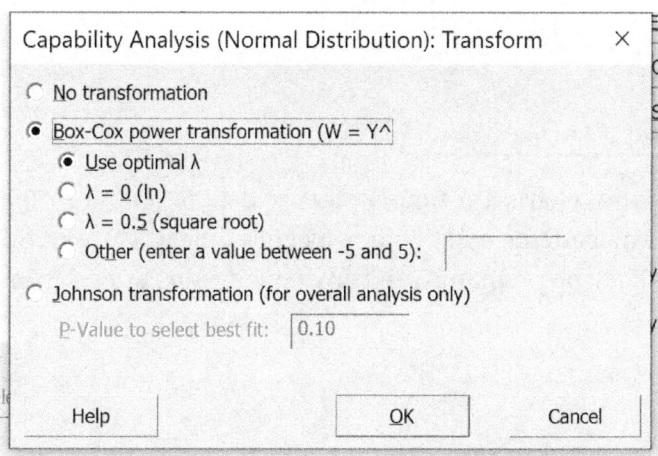

7. Check **Box-Cox Power Transformation** > (choose Use Optimal Lambda)
8. Click **OK** in all dialogue boxes

The output is a capability analysis on the transformed data using spec limits that were also transformed in the same way as the data itself using the same transformation.

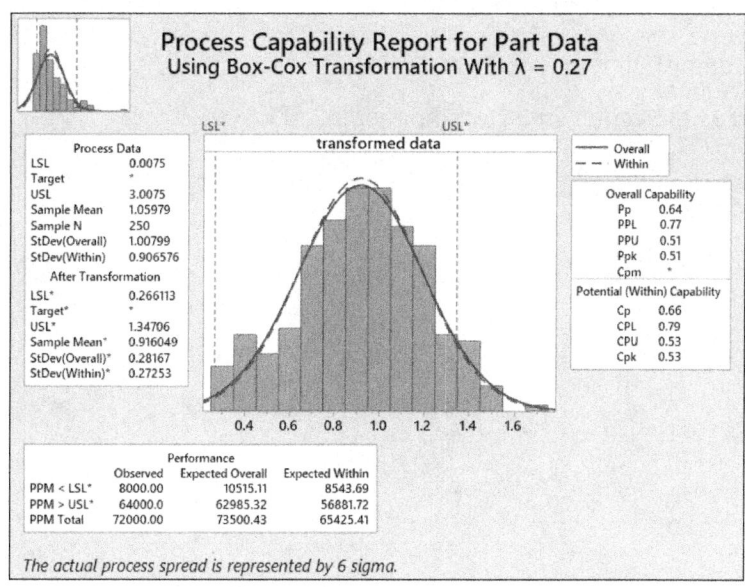

10. PROCESS STABILITY ANALYSIS

10.01 Run Charts Overview

Both run charts and control charts are simply plots of data in order of time. Until you can be reasonably certain that no patterns exist with respect to time, the use of other graphical or descriptive techniques may be premature and any conclusions drawn from those techniques may be misleading.

Purpose

To focus attention on detecting and monitoring process variation over a specified period of time, in recognition that the process is dynamic rather than static;

Separate special cause variation from common cause variation as a guide to management action; and

Identify number of runs about the median (Minitab also studies runs up and down)

Tips for Users

- Collect a minimum of 20 data points
- Plot the median as the center line (not the mean)

10.02 Run Charts with Minitab

1. Choose **Stat > Quality Tools > Run Chart**

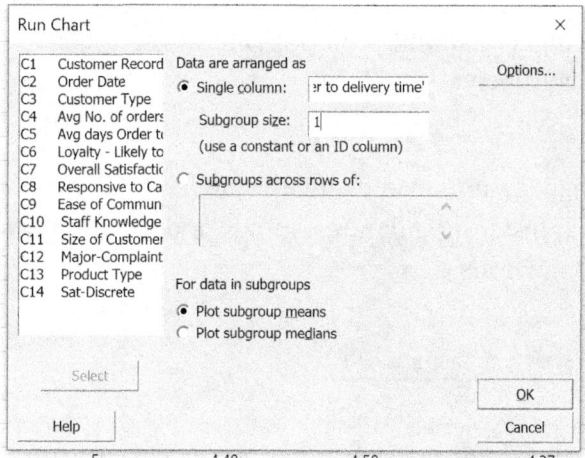

2. **Data are arranged as:** (choose *single column* or *subgroups across rows of*)
3. **Single column:** (insert column and subgroup size) OR **Subgroups across rows of:** (insert relevant columns of data)

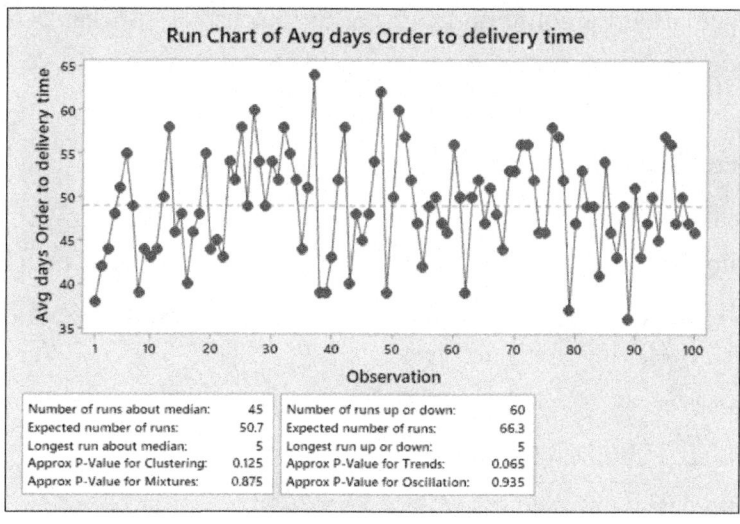

10.03 Using P Values with Run Chart Non Parametric Tests

P Value => α

Where a p value is <u>equal to or greater than</u> the nominated alpha value (α usually = 0.05), you can conclude that a particular situation (clustering, mixtures, trends or oscillation) **does not exist** (with 1 - α level of confidence, i.e. 95%).

P Value < α

Where a p value is <u>less than</u> the nominated alpha value (α usually = 0.05), you can conclude that a particular situation (clustering, mixtures, trends or oscillation) **does exist** (although there is some risk (ie; α) of being wrong).

10.04 Control Charts Overview

<u>Purpose</u>

(1) To focus attention on detecting and monitoring process variation over a specified period of time, in recognition that the process is dynamic rather than static;

(2) To separate **special cause** variation from **common cause** variation as a guide to management action; and

(3) To provide a foundation for common language for discussing process performance.

<u>Using Control Charts</u>

Control charts are employed in four steps.

4. Identify your data type
    - 4.1. Attribute (counting defective units or defects per unit) data; or
    - 4.2. Variables (discrete or continuous numerical variables) data (eg: # of strokes, width of a part, cycle time for a delivery)
5. Select your chart type
    - 5.1. Variable data control charts
    - 5.2. Attribute data control charts
6. Analyse & act upon results
    - 6.1. Test for special causes (see additional tests for X-bar and Individuals Charts)

6.2. Investigate and treat cause

6.3. Update control chart

7. Monitor process performance

Tips for Practitioners

- Collect a minimum of 30 data points
- Investigate special cause variation before treating common cause variation
- Set up Minitab control chart default settings

10.05 Setting Minitab Control Chart Defaults

1. Choose **File > Options**
2. Select the + sign beside **Control Charts and Quality Tools**
3. Choose **Tests**
4. Select **Perform all tests for special causes** (use drop down list)
5. **Test 2:** (change value to 7)
6. **Test 3:** (change value to 7)

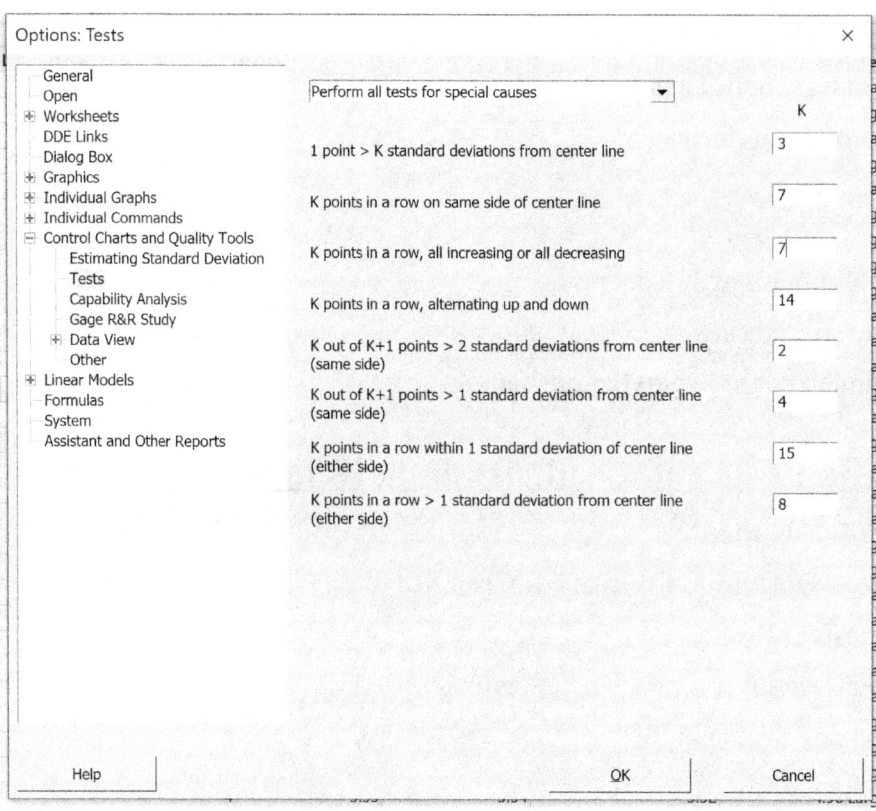

7. Click **OK**

NOTE: You can restore Minitab default settings at any time.

10.06 Choosing The Relevant Control Chart

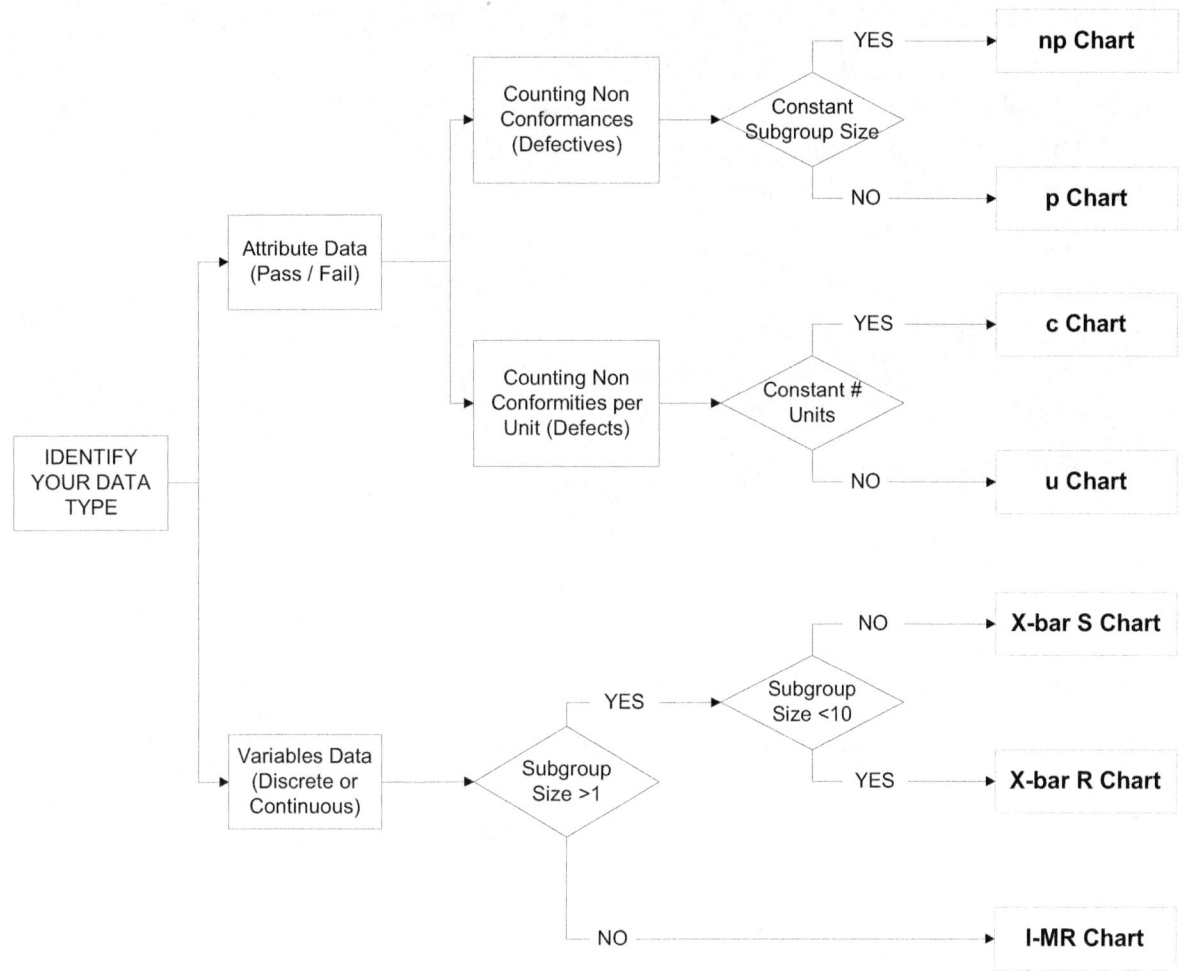

Most Commonly Used Control Charts - Variables Data

Individuals Chart – A chart that plots individual values.

I-MR Chart – A chart that plots individual values and also the moving range of data.

Xbar R Chart – A chart that plots the mean of subgroups and range within subgroups.

Xbar S Chart – A chart that plots the mean of subgroups and standard deviation of subgroups.

Most Commonly Used Control Charts - Attribute Data

np Chart – A chart that plots the relevant number of items in a consistent sized sample or subgroup that are non-conforming or judged to be defective. As the number of non-conforming items is expected to be the proportion (p) times the sample size (n), these are often called np charts. This chart is based on the Binomial Probability Distribution.

p chart – Unlike np charts, this type of chart plots the proportion of units that are defective. They can be used with both equal and unequal sample or subgroup sizes. This chart is based on the Binomial Probability Distribution.

c chart – A chart that plots the relevant count of defects when the subgroup size remains constant. This chart is based on the Poisson Probability Distribution.

u chart – This chart plots the statistic 'u', which is the ratio of number of defects counted to the size of the subgroup. This is used when the size of the subgroup is not consistent. This chart is based on the Poisson Probability Distribution.

10.07 Variable Data - I-MR Chart

Discrete or continuous numerical variables data – subgroup size of 1.
1. Choose **Stat > Control Charts > Variables Charts for Individuals > I-MR**
2. Make **Variables:** cell active
3. Insert column (or multiple columns) of data as required
4. Click **OK** in the dialogue box

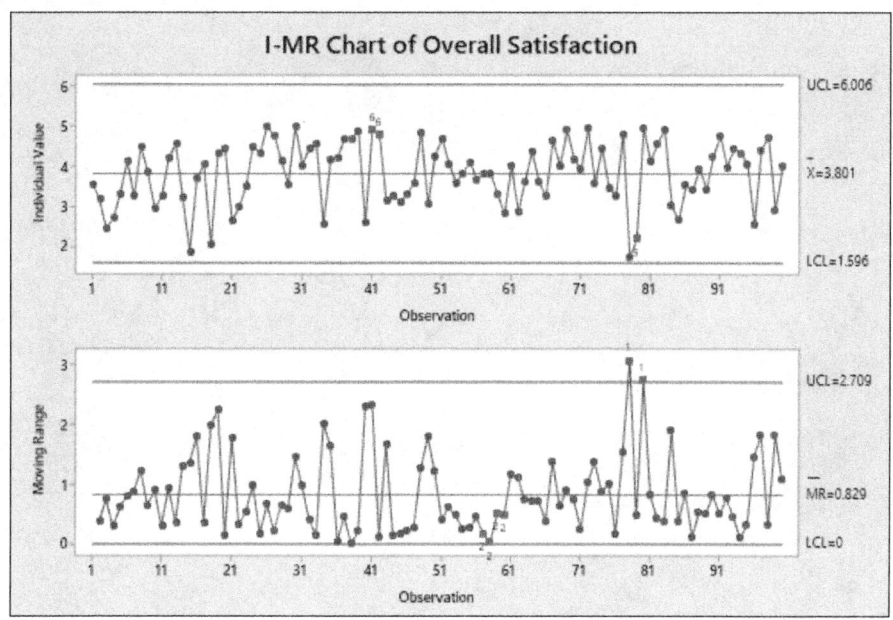

10.08 Variable Data - Xbar-R Chart

Discrete or continuous variables data – subgroup size >1 but <=10.

1. Choose **Stat > Control Charts > Variables Charts for Subgroups > Xbar-R**
2. Choose **All observations for a chart are in one column** (one column of data) OR **All observations for a subgroup are in one row of columns**
3. Insert column or columns of data as required
4. **Subgroup Size:** (enter a numeric subgroup size or insert the column that identifies subgroups). <u>NOTE</u>: This choice does not appear when observations for a subgroup are in one row of columns.
5. Click **OK** in each dialogue box

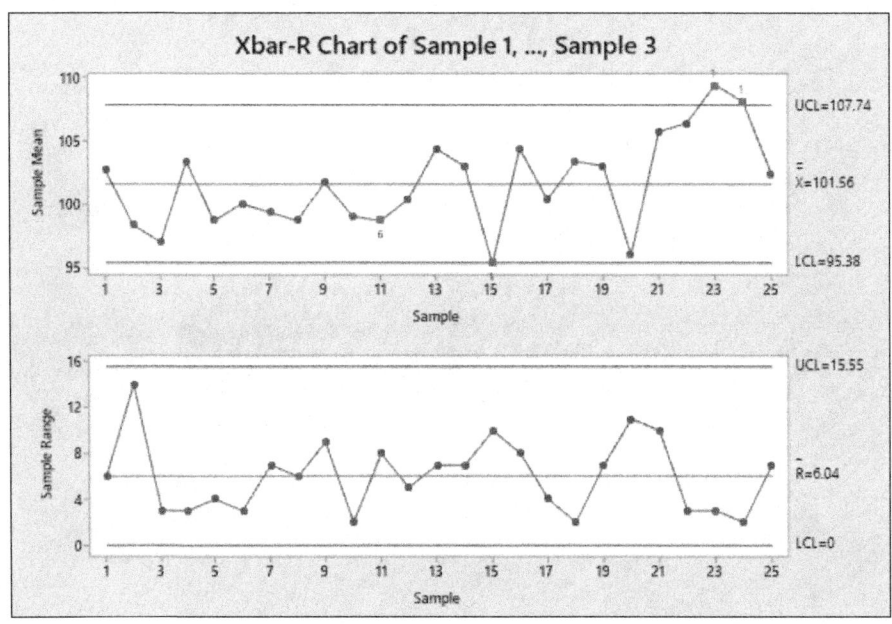

10.09 Variable Data - Xbar-S Chart

Discrete or continuous variables data – subgroup size >10.

1. Choose **Stat > Control Charts > Variables Charts for Subgroups > Xbar-S**
2. Choose **All observations for a chart are in one column** (one column of data) OR **All observations for a subgroup are in one row of columns**
3. Insert column or columns of data as required
4. **Subgroup Size:** (insert numeric subgroup size or column that identifies subgroups) <u>NOTE</u>: This choice does not appear when observations for a subgroup are in one row of columns.
5. Click **OK** in each dialogue box

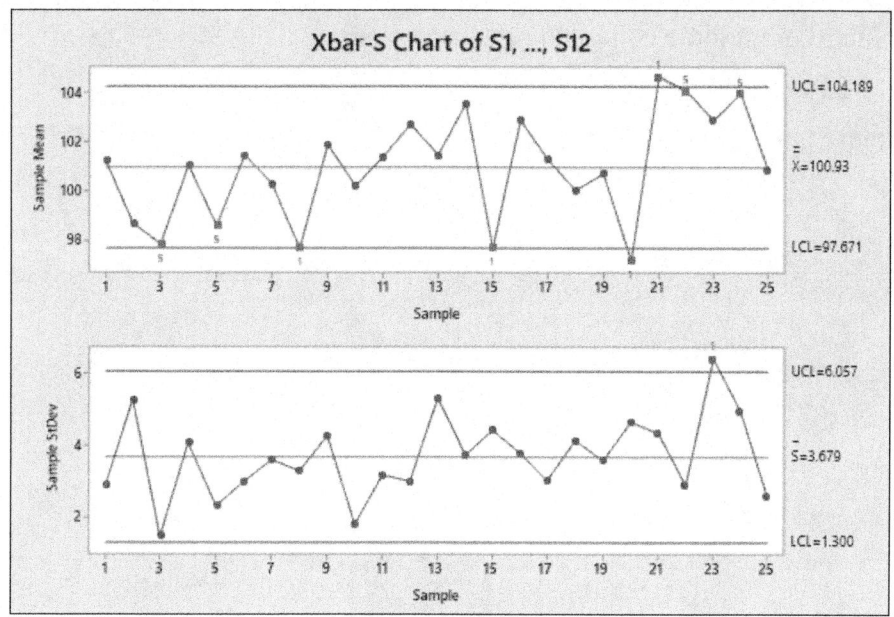

10.10 Variable Data - Separating Data Into Stages on the Same Chart

You can plot your data in control charts and stratify the results using what is referred to as 'stages'.

We use this for plotting more than one population sample on the same chart such as 'before' improvement and 'after' improvement.

I'll show you how it works for the I-MR chart, though you use the same Options tab to do this with any chart.

1. Choose **Stat > Control Charts > Variables Charts for Individuals > I-MR**
5. Make **Variables:** cell active
6. Insert column (or multiple columns) of data as required
2. Choose I-M**R Options …**
3. Select **Stages** tab

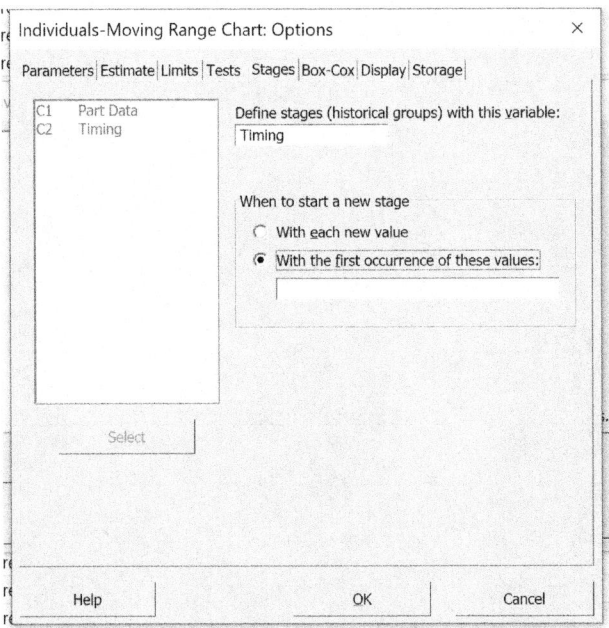

4. **Define stages with this variable:** (insert column with the relevant categories that define the stages by which data will be stratified)

5. **When to start a new stage:** (select)
6. Click **OK** in each dialogue box

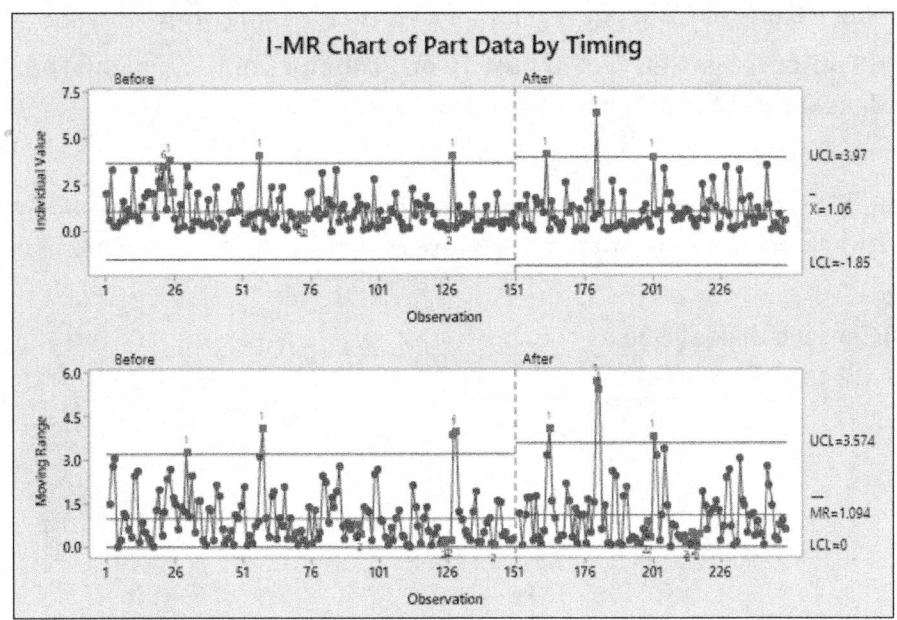

NOTE: This approach can also be used with other control charts.

10.11 Variables Data - Zone Chart

For plotting cumulative scores based on zones 1, 2, & 3 sigmas from mean.

1. Choose **Stat > Control Charts > Variables Charts for Subgroups > Zone**
2. Choose **All observations for a chart are in one column** (one column of data) OR **All observations for a subgroup are in one row of columns**
3. Insert column or columns of data as required
4. **Subgroup Size:** (insert numeric subgroup size or column that identifies subgroups)
   NOTE: This choice does not appear when observations for a subgroup are in one row of columns.
5. Click **OK** in each dialogue box

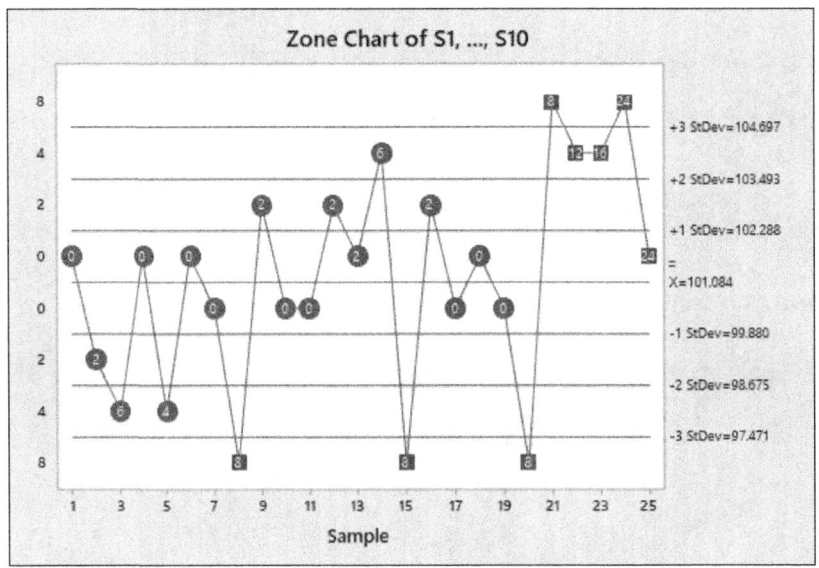

NOTE:

Scores are accumulated for each point in the sequence.

The score is initiated to zero when the mean line is crossed. A score of **8 or more** is highlighted in a red colour and considered to be a point where an out of control situation exists.

Does not require pattern recognition.

10.12 Variables Data - CUSUM Chart

Used for discrete or continuous variables data – subgroup size 1 or more.

A CUSUM Chart plots the cumulative sums (CUSUMs) of the deviations of each sample value from a nominated target value.

Because CUSUM is cumulative, even minor drifting in the process mean will cause steadily increasing or decreasing cumulative deviation values.

To see an example in action, the following is an Individuals chart of a set of process data with a subgroup size of 1 which has a targeted value of 1.00.

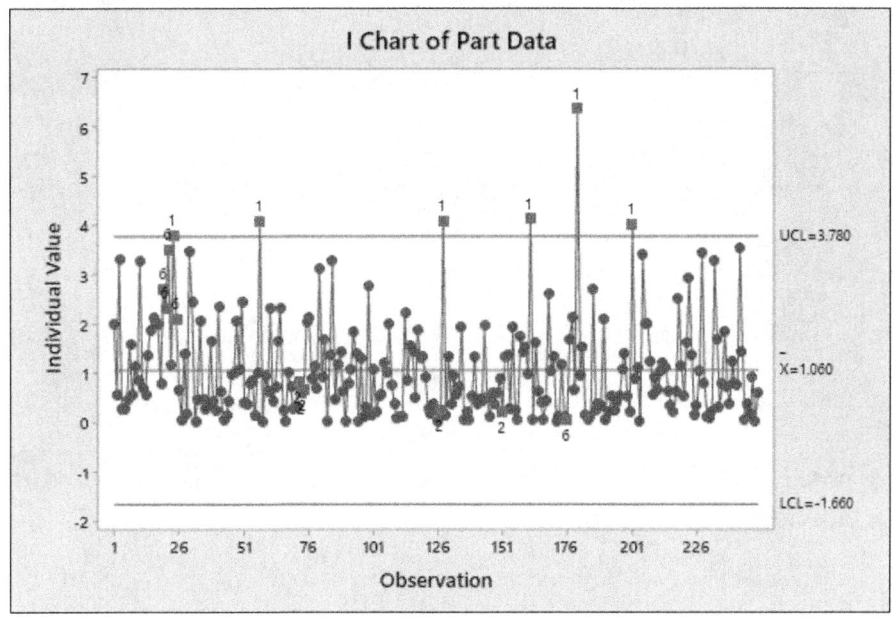

We can plot this same data against the target of 1.00 using the CUSUM chart which looks like this.

1. Choose **Stat > Control Charts > Time-Weighted Charts > CUSUM**
2. Choose **All observations for a chart are in one column** (one column of data) OR **All observations for a subgroup are in one row of columns**
3. Insert column or columns of data as required

4. **Subgroup Size:** (insert numeric subgroup size or column that identifies subgroups)
   NOTE: This choice does not appear when observations for a subgroup are in one row of columns.

5. Click **OK** in each dialogue box

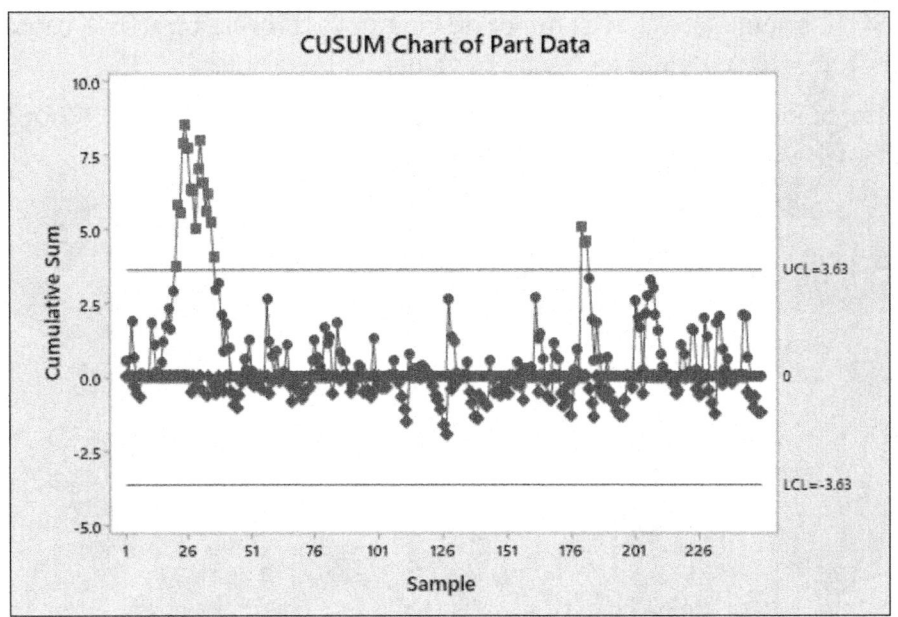

We can see the process is drifting upwards in its early stages which is not necessarily that obvious in the Individuals chart.

10.13 Adding Reference Lines to Control Charts

Reference lines such as customer specification limits can be added to control charts for analysis purposes. For example, in the example below, the customer has an upper specification limit of 3.5 days and lower specification limit of 2.5 days.

1. Right click the chart (ie: **Xbar** or **Individuals**)
2. Choose **Edit Graph**
3. From the now viewable edit menu, select **Add Item > Reference Lines**
4. **Show reference lines for Y positions:** (insert reference line values – customer specification limits – can be a single reference line or multiple reference lines)
5. Click **OK** in each dialogue box

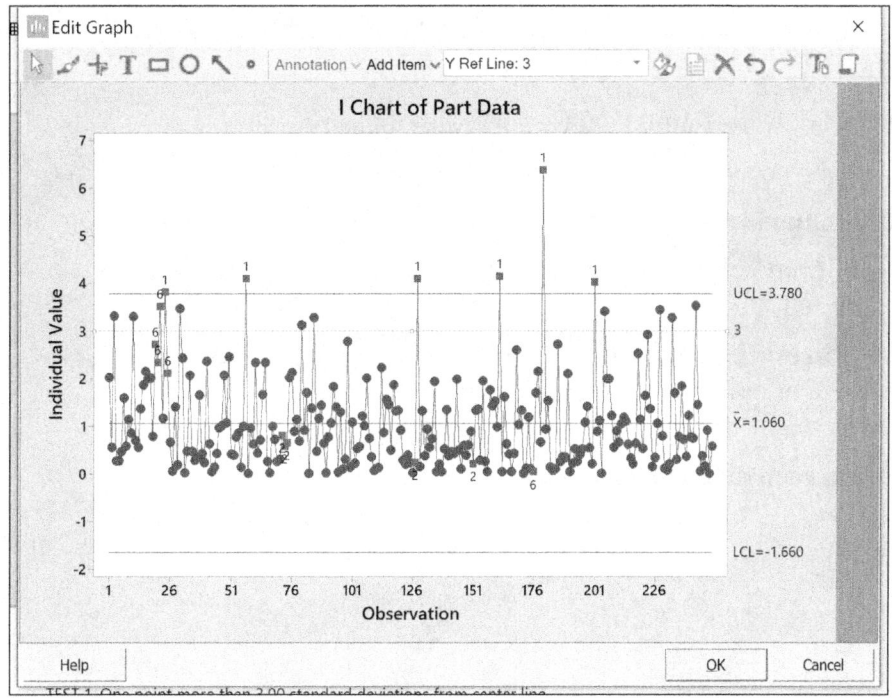

10.14 Attribute Data - NP Chart

Count (number of defective units) data – constant sample size.

1. Choose **Stat > Control Charts > Attributes Charts > NP**
2. **Variables:** Insert column or columns of data as required
3. **Subgroup Sizes:** (insert numeric subgroup size or column that identifies subgroups)
4. Click **OK** in each dialogue box

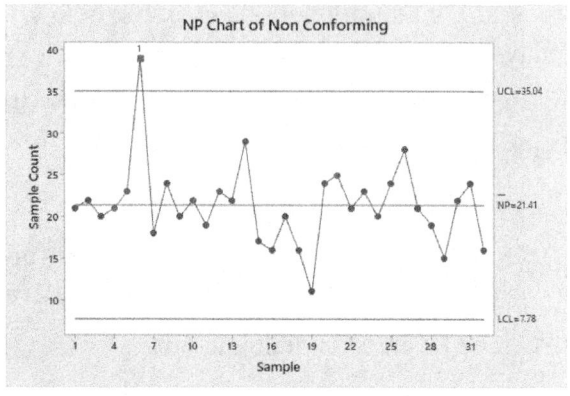

10.15 Attribute Data - P Chart

Count (number of defective units) data – non-constant sample size.

1. Choose **Stat > Control Charts > Attributes Charts > P**
2. **Variables:** Insert column or columns of data as required
3. **Subgroup Sizes:** (insert numeric subgroup size or column that identifies subgroups)
4. Click **OK** in each dialogue box

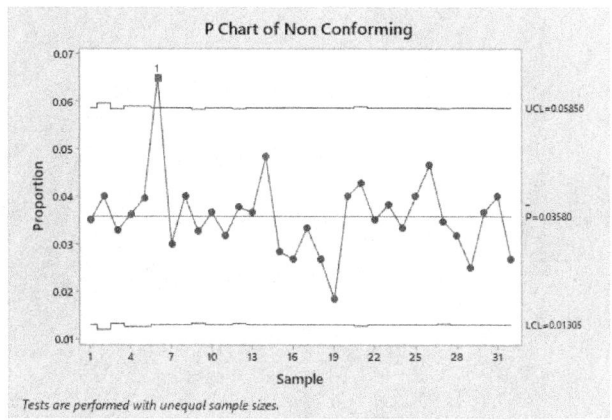

10.16 Attribute Data - U Chart

Count (number of defects per unit) data – non-constant number of units.

1. Choose **Stat > Control Charts > Attributes Charts > U**
2. **Variables:** Insert column or columns of data as required
3. **Subgroup Sizes:** (insert numeric subgroup size or column that identifies subgroups)
4. Click **OK** in each dialogue box

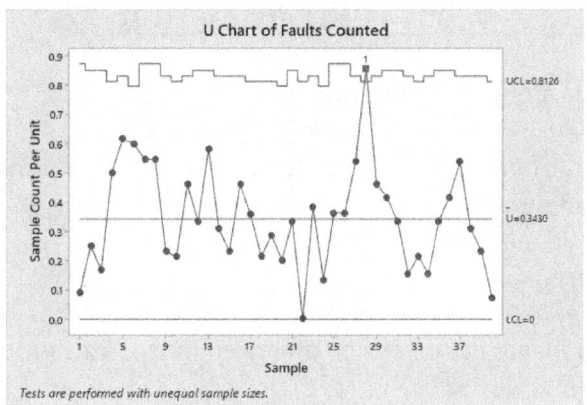

10.17 Attribute Data - C Chart

Count (number of defects per unit) data – defects – constant number of units.

1. Choose **Stat > Control Charts > Attributes Charts > C**
2. **Variables:** Insert column or columns of data as required
3. Click **OK** in each dialogue box

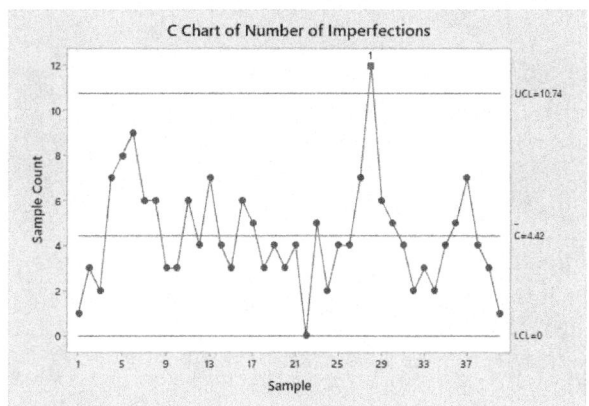

11. STRATIFYING DATA - SOURCES OF VARIATION

11.01 What is Stratification

The Concept of Stratification

Stratification is nothing more than slicing and dicing data into different pieces or chunks or categories.

Purpose

To locate the existence of any source of variation / waste / the problem.

Stratification Tools for Visualising Differences

Some of the most commonly used stratification tools used by continual improvement professionals include:

Box Plots - Pareto Charts

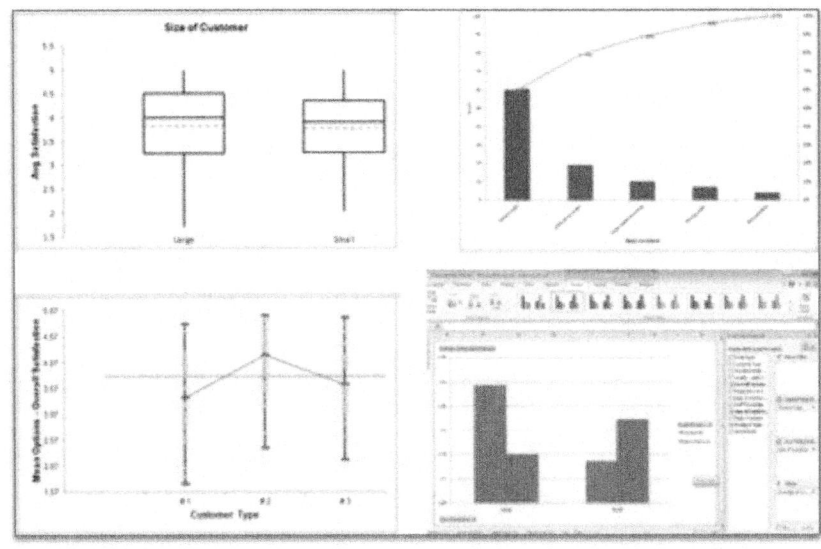

Multi Vari Charts - Pivot Charts

These visual tools give you a sense of difference. In most cases however, they do not validate whether or not the difference you see is significant enough to say it is not a sampling error.

That's where more comprehensive statistical tools come into play.

Stratification Tools for Validating Differences

In most cases we use Hypothesis Tests to validate the significance of any difference we observe. These are covered fully later in the book.

A new tool is now emerging - the ANOM Chart - which is gaining popularity in the improvement world when stratifying data and confirming whether or not any difference is significant.

We'll take a look at these over the following pages.

11.02 Stratified Pie Charts

1. Click **Graph > Pie Chart**
2. Select **'Chart counts of unique values'** (if data you are counting is in a single column)
3. Make the **Categorical variables:** cell active
4. Select and **insert column of interest** (the data you will count)
5. To stratify the pie chart, select **Multiple Graphs**

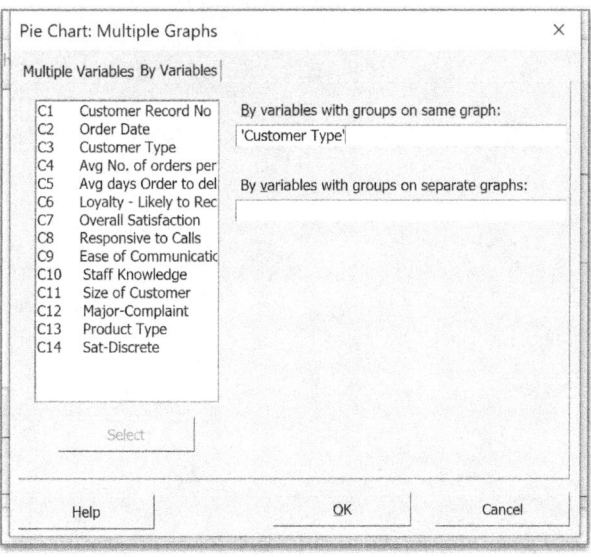

6. Select the '**By Variables**' tab

7. Insert column (or columns for multiple levels of stratification) to stratify data
8. Click **OK**
9. Select **Labels**
10. Select **Slice Labels** tab
11. Choose labels you want to display
12. Click **OK** in all dialogue boxes

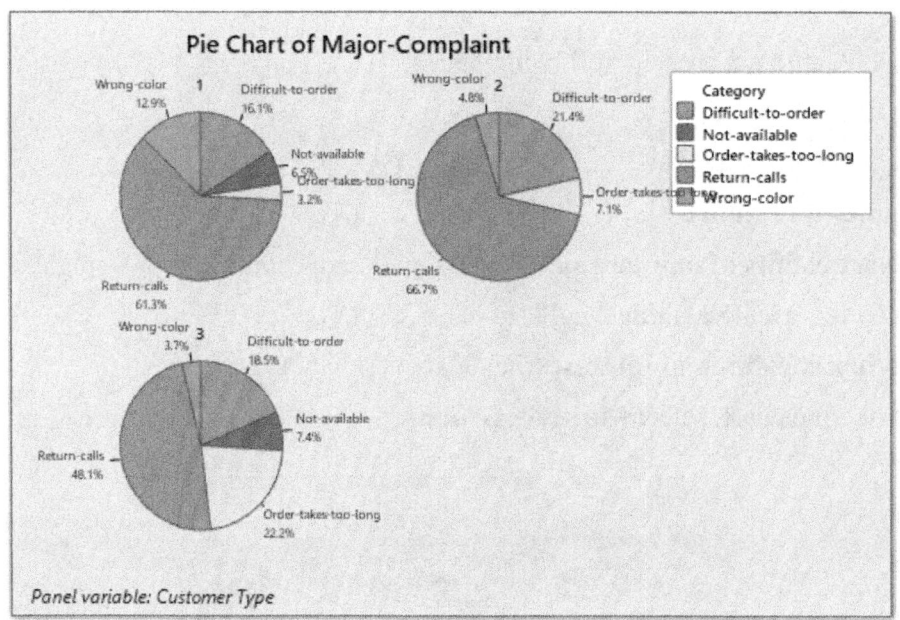

11.03 Stratified Histograms

1. Click **Graph > Histogram**
2. Select **'With Fit and Groups'** (fitted normal curve might help you distinguish)
3. Click **OK**

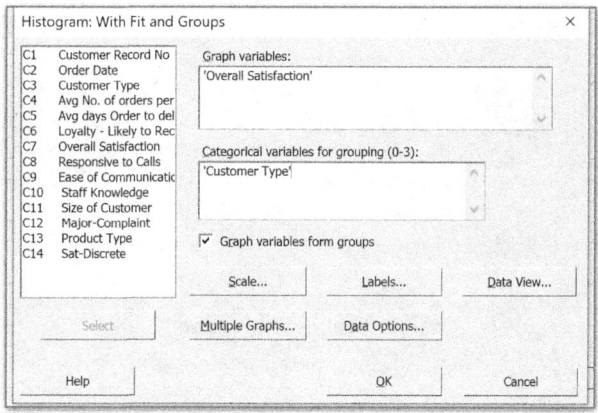

4. Make the **Graph variables:** cell active
5. Select and insert **Column of interest**
6. Make the **Categorical variables for grouping (0-3):** cell active
7. Select and insert **Column of interest**
8. Click **OK**

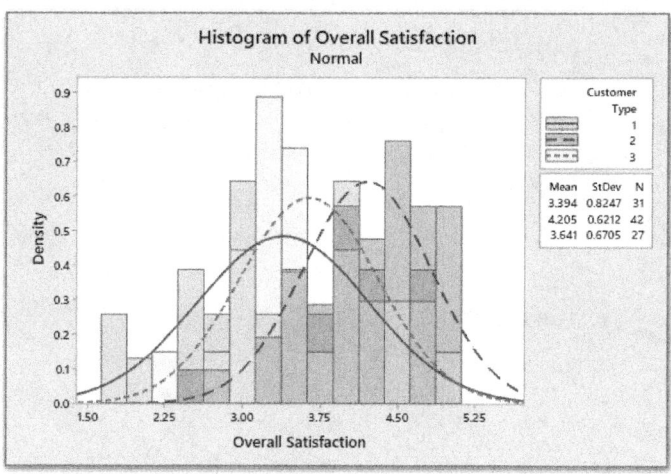

11.04 Stratified Boxplots - Single Y

1. Click **Graph > Boxplot**
2. Select **'With Groups'** (when you want to stratify a single Y)
3. Click **OK**

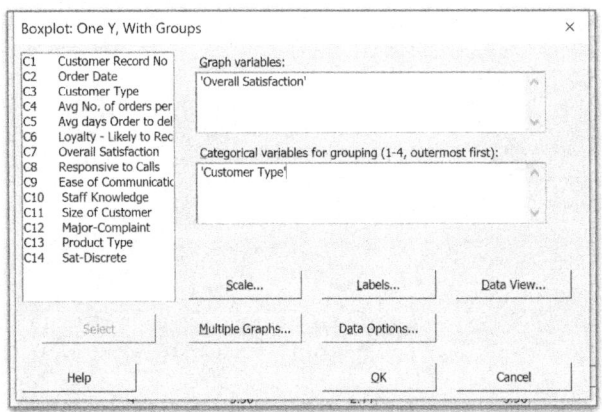

4. Make the **Graph variables:** cell active
5. Select and insert column containing the variable of interest
6. Make the **Categorical variable for grouping:** cell active
7. Select and insert the categorical variable to stratify the data
8. Click **OK**

11.05 ANOM Chart for Means - Normal Data Only

Used to visually compare 'means' for data that is *normally distributed* only.

1. Click **Stat > ANOVA > Analysis of Means..**

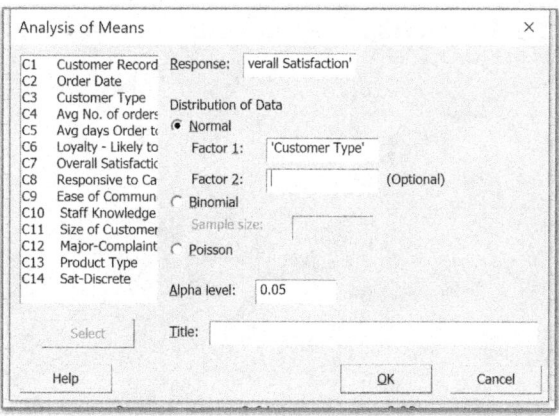

2. Make the **Response:** cell active and insert the column with the Y data

3. Make the **Factor 1:** cell active and insert the column containing the categorical variable of interest (this is a one-way analysis)

4. (Optional) Make the **Factor 2:** cell active and insert the column containing the 2nd categorical variable of interest (this is now a two-way analysis)

5. Click **OK**

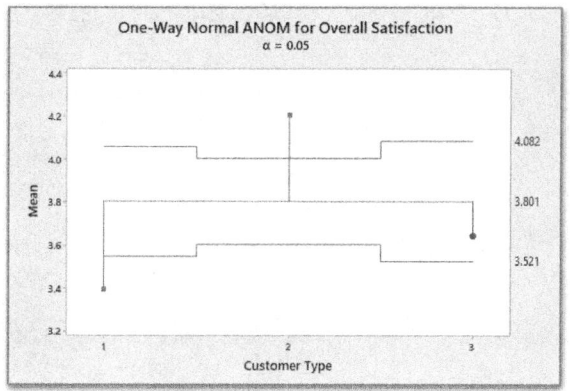

11.06 ANOM Chart for Binomial and Poisson Data

Binomial Data is collected when you count the number of defective units from samples of the same size. For example - you inspected 100 paper rolls each day and counted how many were *defective units* each day.

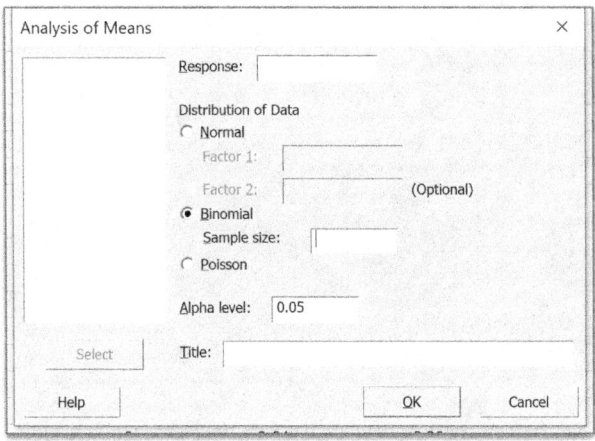

Poisson Data is collected when you count the number of defects (not defective units) from samples of the same size. For example - you inspected 100 paper rolls each day and counted the number of *defects* you found each day in 100 rolls.

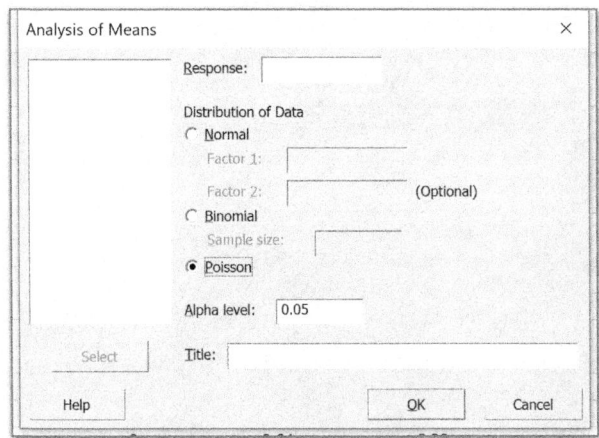

11.07 Stratification with Pivot tables / Pivot Charts

Pivot Table with MS Excel (Version 2016)

The File: pt-safety-data.xlsx

1. Activate one cell within the data area of the worksheet.
2. Select **Insert > Pivot Table > From Table/Range**

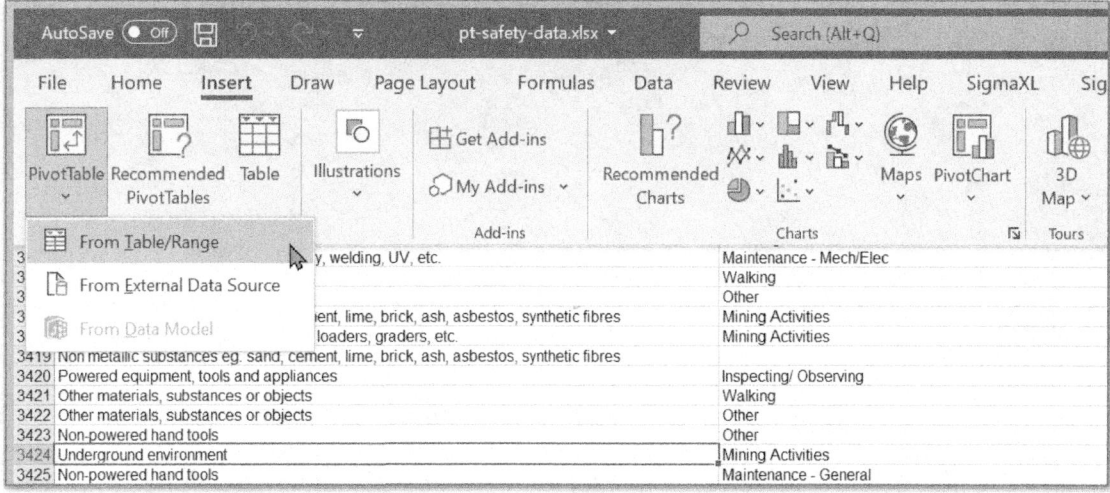

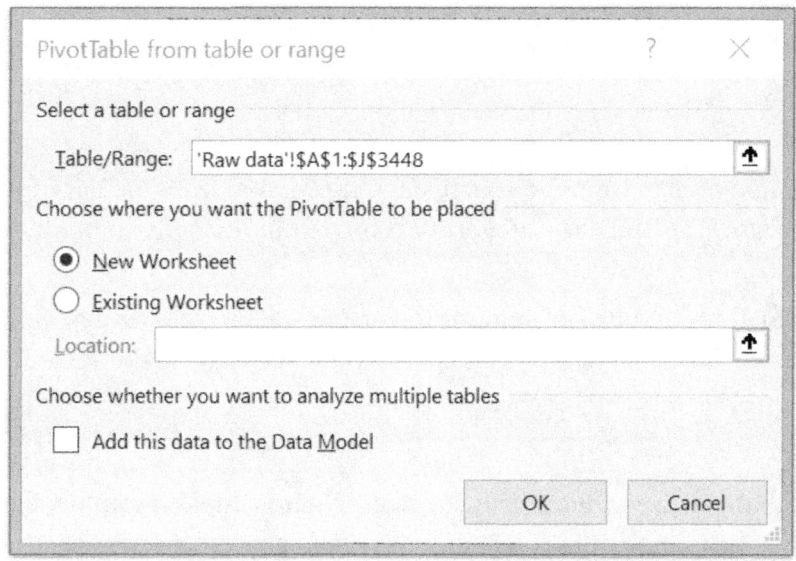

3. Check **OK**

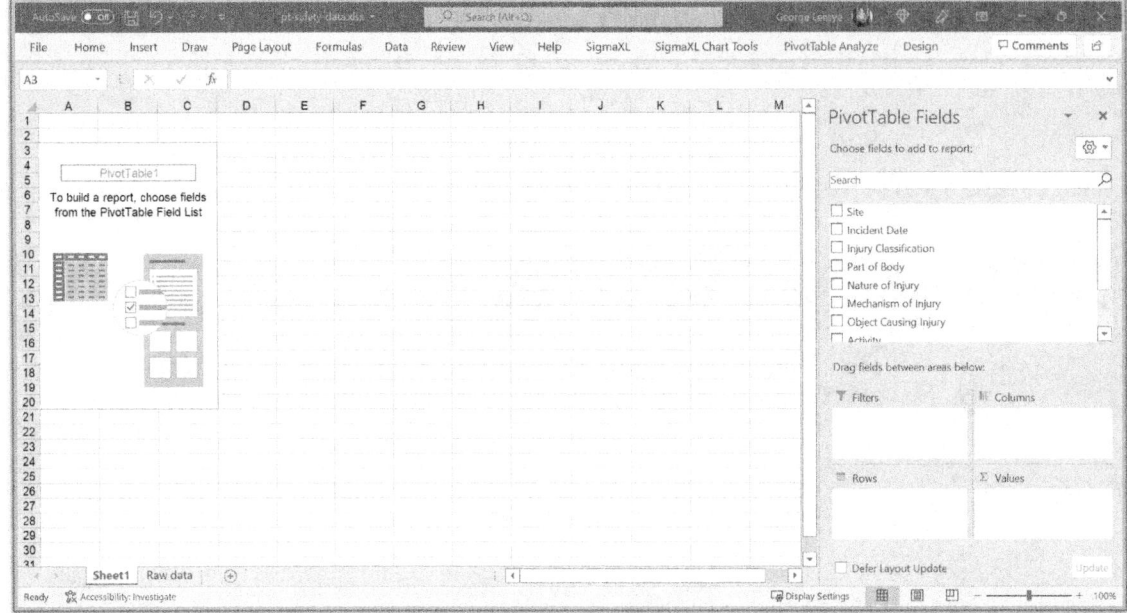

That creates the basis for the Pivot Table.

In order to create the actual Pivot Table in later versions of Excel, you need to be familiar with the specific terms used in the Pivot Table Fields area.

An example of what we are referring to is provided at the end of this section.

Fields

A field is a collection of data from the source data. It is drawn from the data column headings and can comprise any type of data - categorical (e.g. part of the body injured), numerical (eg. number of days off work), dates etc.

To set up our Pivot Table and Pivot Chart, or to change what we are analysing, we simply drag these into the areas below. Where they go depends on what you want to look at.

Filters

A filter is a field that you use to filter data by specific items. In the example, the Site field allows you to view data for all sites together, or select one or more specific sites.

It dictates what the overall Pivot Chart shows.

Refer to the example Pivot Chart shown at the end of this section where the chart shows results for all sites.

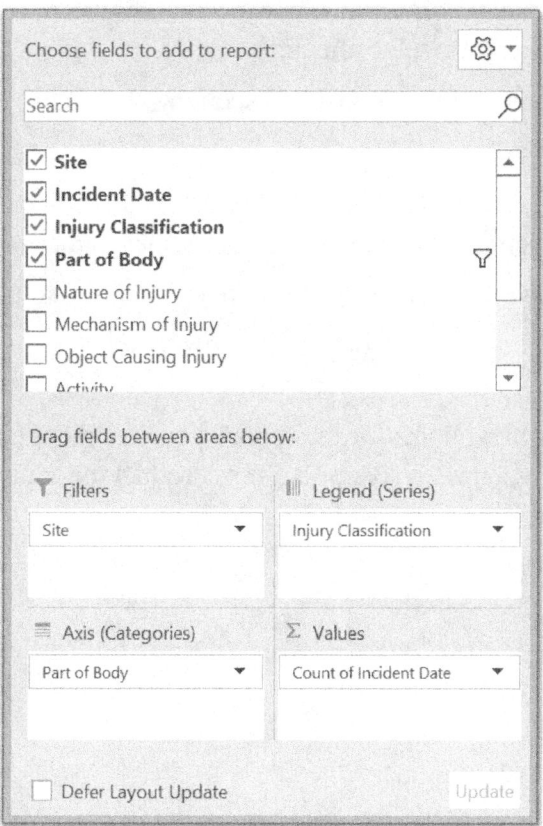

Rows / Axis (Categories)

This controls what is shown across a chart, for example when the field 'Part of the Body' is placed here, it dictates how the chart is stratified.

For example if we create a column chart as our Pivot Chart, this would dictate what the columns would refer to, in this case various parts of the body.

Refer to the example shown at the end of this section.

Columns / Legend (Series)

The items in the field dictate the individual data series. In the example, there are 5 different injury classifications, so if we were counting number of injuries and displaying these as a column chart showing the counts for various body parts, this field would stratify each of those columns and show counts by injury classification.

Refer to the Pivot Chart shown at the end of this section.

Σ Values

This is a field from the underlying source data that provides values to compare or measure.

In the example, we've added the Incident Date field and set it up to Count events.

So the values being displayed in the Pivot Chart in this case will be a count of events for each element in the chart.

Depending on the source data you use for the report, you can change the summary function from the default setting of 'Count' to Average, Sum, Product, or some other calculation.

11.08 Setting Up The Pivot Chart

1. Select **PivotTable Analyse > PivotChart**

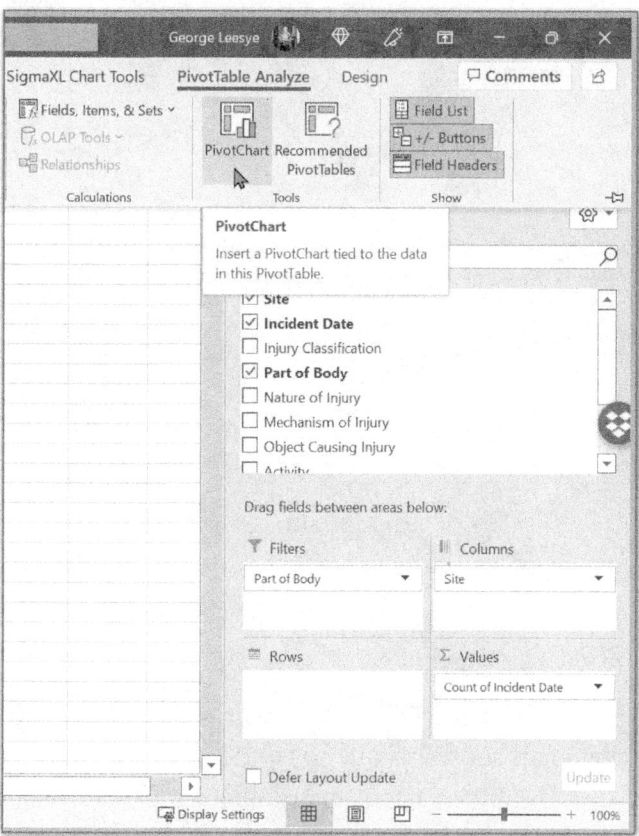

2. Choose the Chart Type you want
3. Click **OK**

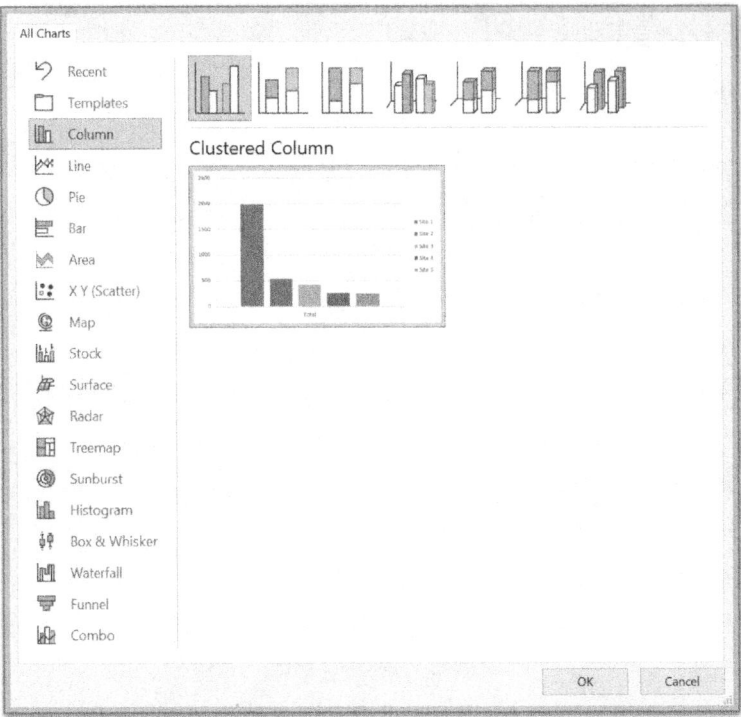

Pivot Chart Example

You'll then see a chart placed on to the Pivot Table worksheet which is based on how you set up your fields. The following chart shows what one would see using the field choices shown in the image earlier where we discussed the various areas and terms of a Pivot Table.

MINITAB STATISTICAL ANALYSIS HANDBOOK - VERSION 21

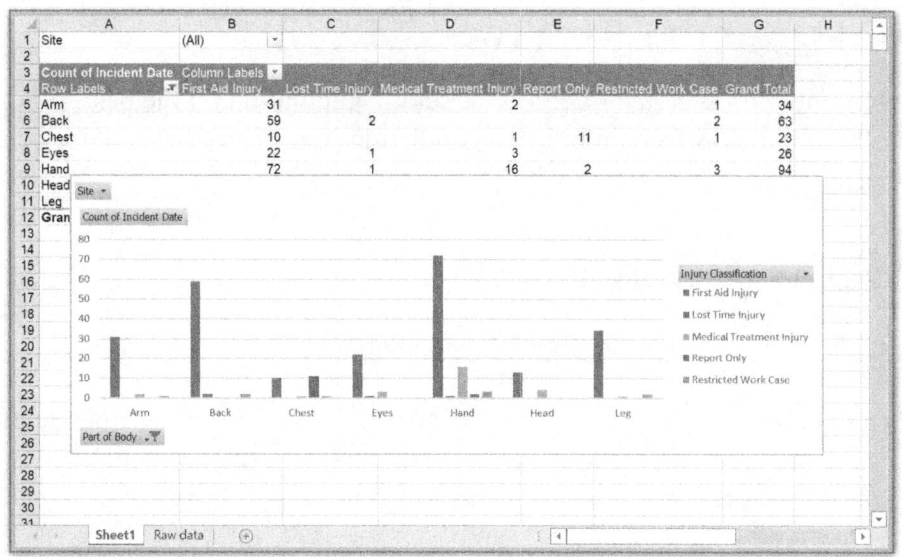

12. HYPOTHESIS TESTING OVERVIEW

Used when we want to make some inference about the population on the basis of a sample. Hence you will notice the use of symbols for population parameters (μ) and not sample statistics (x-bar).

12.01 The Hypothesis Testing Process

STEP 1 - State the 'Null Hypothesis' about the population.

Null Hypothesis is always a statement of no difference. So we would hypothesise that there is no differences between proportions (π), means (μ) or variances (σ^2) of populations, or the mean (μ) equals a specific number.

STEP 2 - State the 'Alternative Hypothesis' about the population.

A 2 sided test = parameters are not equal.

A 1 sided test = one parameter is greater or less than the other.

STEP 3 - State the significance level 'alpha'

The level of risk in concluding that the null hypothesis is false when in fact it is true – typically 0.05.

STEP 4 - Choose the right test

(refer to table on following page)

STEP 5 - Test all assumptions for the test chosen

Assumptions are listed with each of the tests in this handbook, they describe what criteria must be met before each tool can be used.

STEP 6 - Compute the test statistic and its P value

The p-value is used to make a decision about which hypothesis (null or alternative) to reject or not reject.

STEP 7 - State your conclusions

Conclusions are drawn based on the p-value decision, and should be written scientifically. However good practitioners can write them as well in plain English that can be understood by non- statistical people.

12.02 Choosing Hypothesis Tests – Decision Flowchart

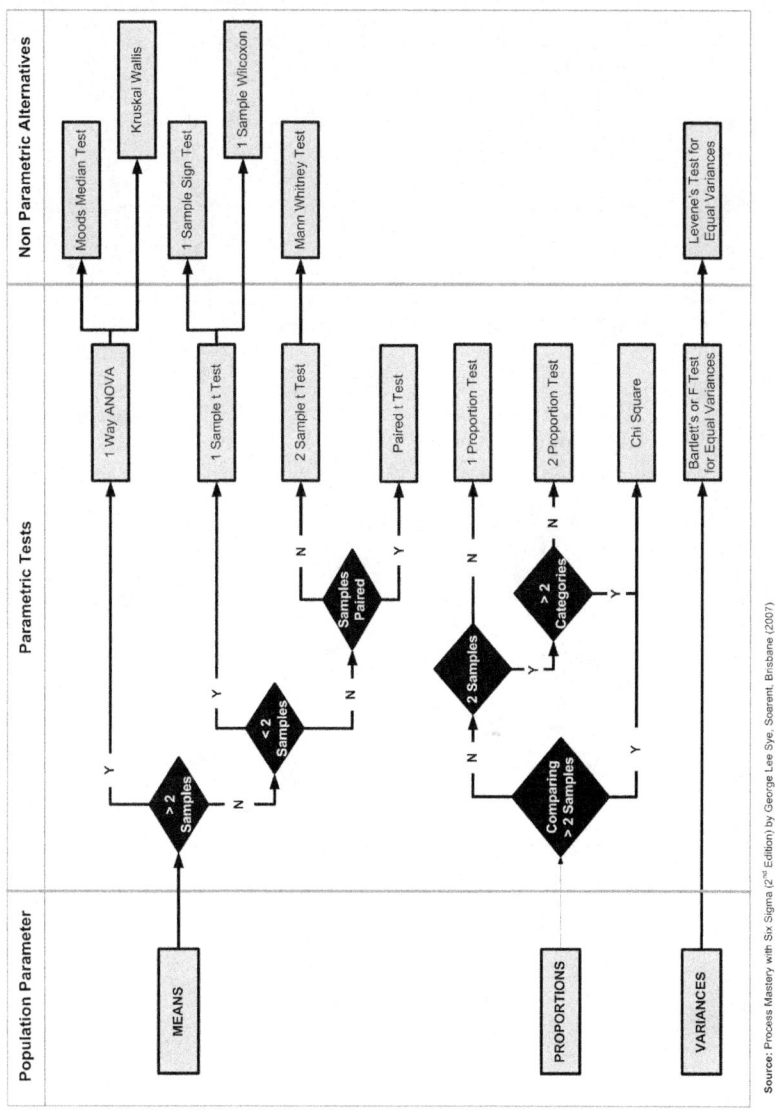

12.03 Summary of Hypothesis Testing Tools

The table below offers a summary of the most common tests and relevant assumptions.

Test	Parameter	Used when looking for differences ...	Assumptions
Chi-Square	Proportions	In proportions between 2 or more samples.	Counts in each cell ≥ 5
1 Proportion Test	Proportions	Between a single proportion of a sample and a target proportion.	Binomial Proportions Independent sample
2 Proportion Test	Proportions	Between a single proportion of two independent samples.	Binomial Proportions Independent sample
1 Sample t Test	Means	Between mean of a sample and a target mean.	Normal sample means
2 Sample t Test	Means	Between means of two independent samples.	Independent samples Normal sample means Equal Variances (desirable)
Paired t Test	Means	Between means of two paired samples.	Paired data (by some factor) Normal sample means
1 Way ANOVA	Means	Between means of more than two independent samples.	Independent samples - Independence of Error (residuals) Normal Distribution - Normality of Error (residuals) Equal Variances - Constant Error Variance
Test for Equal Variances	Variances	Among variances of two or more independent samples.	Independent samples Normally distributed data (use Bartlett's test)
1 Sample Sign Test	Medians	Between median of a sample and a target median.	
Mann Whitney Test	Medians	Between medians of two independent samples.	Independent samples
Moods Median Test	Medians	Between medians of two or more independent samples.	Independent samples Populations have same shaped distributions Equal Variances

13. HYPOTHESIS TESTING TOOLS IN DETAIL

13.01 Stating Hypothesis Test Conclusions

Conclusions are worded according to the type of decision-making risk that exists. Our conclusion will comprise three parts:

1. A reference to the P value and α value;
2. A statement as to whether the null hypothesis is *rejected* or *not rejected*; and
3. A final concluding statement with reference to the parameter under analysis.

P value => α:

- Since the P value of 0.___ is greater than / equal to α (0.05), we do not reject the null hypothesis, and conclude with 95% confidence (1 - α x 100) that (insert reference to H_O).

P value < α:

- Since the P value of 0.___ is less than α (0.05), we reject the null hypothesis at the 0.05 significance level (α), and conclude that (insert reference to H_A).

13.02 Chi-Square Test for Association

Used to test hypothesise about proportions from multiple samples. (e.g. Proportion of different types of safety injuries across multiple business units)

Counts for each cell are ideally > 5.

The Null and Alternative Hypothesis for Chi Square testing is:

H_0: The proportions are equal
H_A: The proportions are not equal

Data in Two-Way Table Format

Used when counts are recorded in a table:
- rows are levels of one factor (eg: work site)
- columns are the levels of the other factor (eg: safety incident type)

RESULTS	SITE A	SITE B	SITE C	SITE D	TOTALS
Hand Injuries	30	48	112	12	202
Eye Injuries	20	30	69	8	127

1. Choose **Stat > Tables > Chi-Square Test for Association**

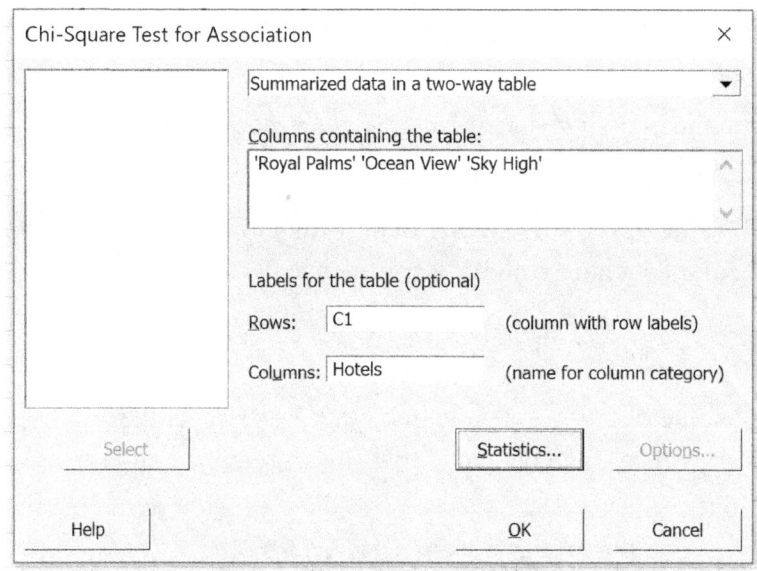

2. Select **Summarised data in a two-way table** layout
3. **Columns containing the table:** (insert relevant columns)
4. **Rows:** (insert any column that has the labels for rows)
5. **Columns:** (you name the column category)
6. Click **OK**

⊞ TWO WAY TABLE
Chi-Square Test for Association: C1, Hotels

Rows: C1   Columns: Hotels

	Royal Palms	Ocean View	Sky High	All
Price	23	7	37	67
	31.53	11.82	23.65	
Location	39	13	8	60
	28.24	10.59	21.18	
Room	13	5	13	31
	14.59	5.47	10.94	
Other	13	8	8	29
	13.65	5.12	10.24	
All	88	33	66	187

Cell Contents
  Count
  Expected count

Chi-Square Test

	Chi-Square	DF	P-Value
Pearson	27.410	6	0.000
Likelihood Ratio	28.762	6	0.000

Data in Raw Categorical Format (not counted)

Counts are not recorded. Categorical data is stored in stacked columns:

Column 1 consists of observations associated with one factor (eg: work site by name)

Column 2 consists of observations associated with the other factor (eg: safety incident type)

Stacked categorical data in raw format looks like that shown in the example on the right.

Nothing has been counted, it's simply raw data.

⇩	C1-T	C2-T
	Work Site	Injury Type
1	A	Head
2	A	Eye
3	B	Eye

4	C	Other
5	C	Head
6	D	Head
7	D	Eye
8	A	Other

1. Choose **Stat > Tables > Chi-Square Test for Association**
2. Select **Raw data (categorical variables)** layout

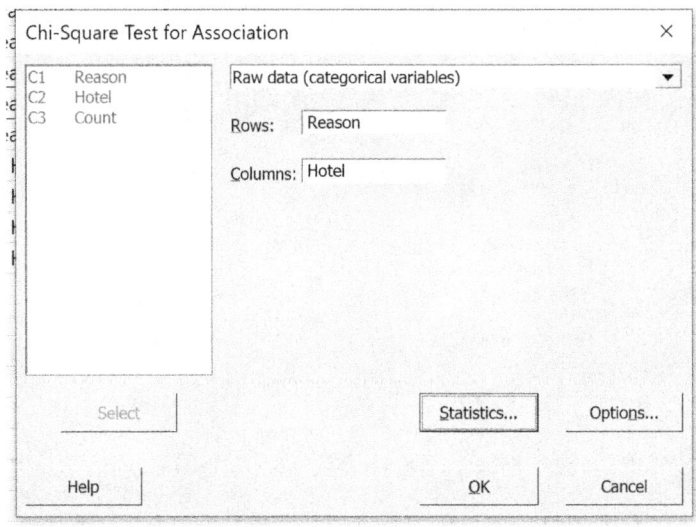

3. **Rows:** (insert column containing the categories that define the rows of the table)
4. **Columns:** (insert the column that contains the categories that define the columns of the table)
5. Click **OK** in all dialogue boxes

<u>Data in Stacked Column Format (with summary counts)</u>

Counts are recorded and categorical data is stored in stacked columns:

Column 1 consists of observations associated with one factor (eg: work site by name)

Column 2 consists of observations associated with the other factor (eg: safety incident type)

Column 3 holds the counts for each combination of categories

Stacked categorical data in raw format looks like that shown in the example on the right.

Nothing has been counted, it's simply raw data.

⇩	C1-T	C2-T	C3
	Work Site	Injury Type	Count
1	A	Head	23
2	A	Eye	42
3	B	Eye	26
4	C	Other	45
5	C	Head	44
6	D	Head	25
7	D	Eye	18
8	A	Other	16

1. Choose **Stat > Tables > Cross Tabulation and Chi-Square**
2. Select **Raw data (categorical variables)** layout
3. **Rows:** (insert column containing the categories that define the rows of the table)
4. **Columns:** (insert the column that contains the categories that define the columns of the table)
5. **Frequencies:** (insert the column that contains the summary counts)

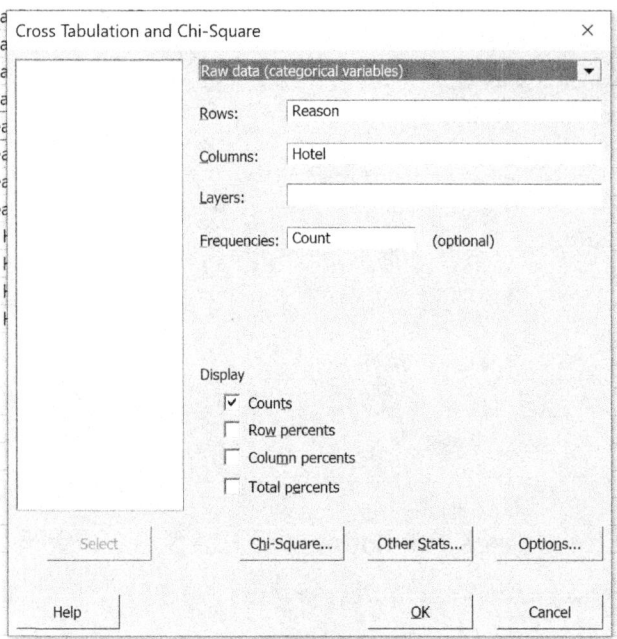

6. Select **Chi-Square..**

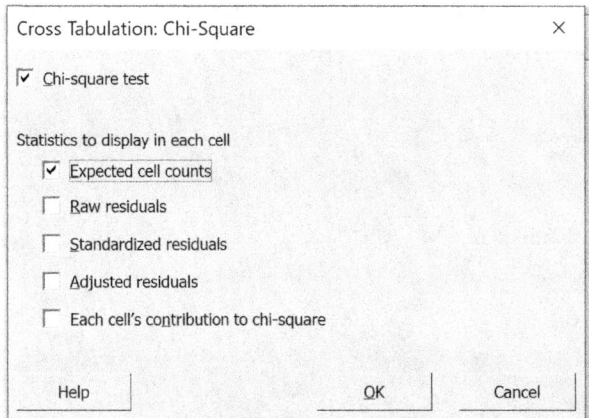

7. Check **Chi-square test** and **Expected cell counts** (so you run the test and not just create a table of actual counts)
8. Click **OK** in all dialogue boxes

13.03 1 Proportion Test

Used to test hypothesis about a single population proportion based on data from a random sample. (e.g. you want to determine if the proportion of defects from your process is better or worse than the industry average)

The Null and Alternative Hypothesis for 1 Proportion testing is:

> **H₀**: The proportion is = to a target value
>
> **Hₐ**: The proportion is (< ≠ >) to a target value

1. Choose **Stat > Basic Statistics > 1 Proportion**
2. OPTION 1 - **One or m samples, each in columns:** (insert relevant columns)

NOTE: If you are going to insert samples from columns, each cell of the column must contain one of two possible values and correspond to a single item or subject. The possible values in these columns have to be exactly the same if you are going to enter multiple columns

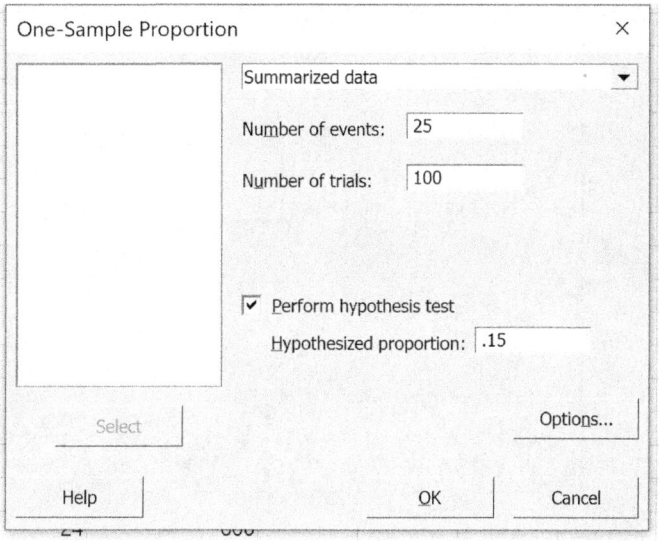

3. OPTION 2 - **Summarised Data:**
   a. **Number of events** - Enter the number of observed events of interest. Incidentally, you can enter more than one value.
   b. **Number of trials** - Enter a single value for the number of trials which in many cases will be the sample size.
4. Select **Perform hypothesis test** (insert the Hypothesised proportion in the cell provided)

5. Select **Options**

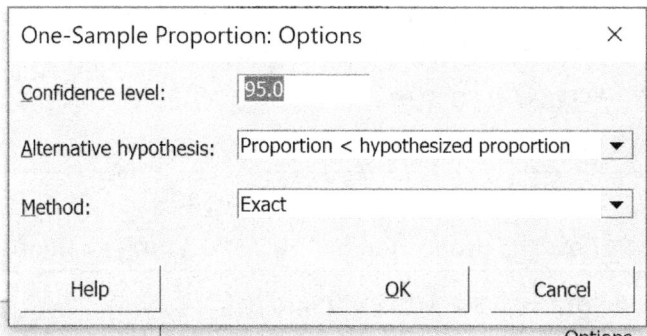

6. **Alternative** - Choose the form of the alternative hypothesis: less than, not equal, or greater than. Remember that if you choose a less than (lower-tailed test) or a greater than (upper-tailed test), only an upper or lower confidence bound will be constructed, as opposed to a confidence interval.

7. Click **OK**

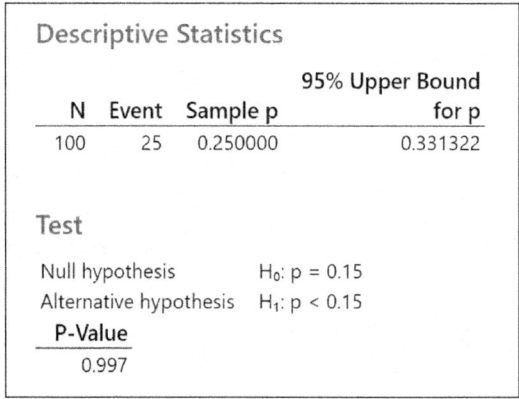

13.04 2 Proportion Test

Used to test hypothesis about the binomial proportions from two populations based on data from random samples. (e.g. you want to determine if the proportion of defects from Production Line 1 is better or worse than Production Line 2)

The Null and Alternative Hypothesis for 2 Proportion testing is:

> H_0: The proportions of sample 1 = the proportions of sample 2
>
> H_A: The proportions of sample 1 is ($< \neq >$) the proportions of sample 2

1. Choose **Stat > Basic Statistics > 2 Proportions**

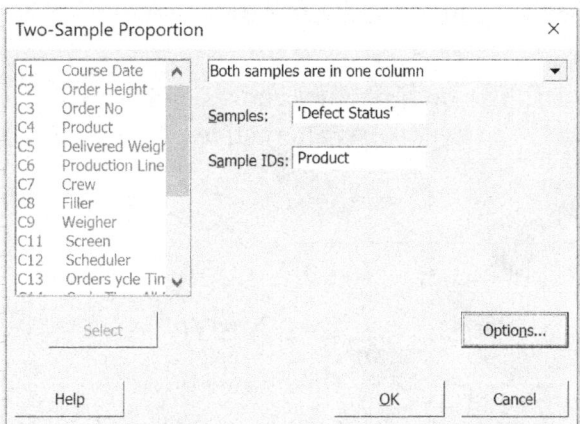

2. OPTION 1 - **Both samples are in one column:** (insert relevant columns)
    a. **Samples** – Enter the column containing the raw data to be analysed.
    b. **Subscripts** – Enter the column that identifies the sample subscripts (i.e. line 1 and line 2).
3. OPTION 2 – **Each sample in its own column:** (enter the columns that contain the two samples under analysis – remember the order of insertion is important when you select less than and greater than alternative hypothesis)
4. OPTION 3 – **Summarised Data:**
    a. **Events** - Enter the number of observed events of interest for each sample.
    b. **Trials** - Enter a single value for the number of trials for each sample which in most cases will be the sample size.
5. Select **Options**

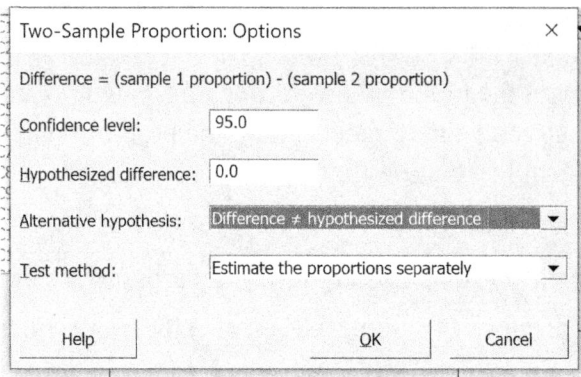

6. **Alternative** - Choose the form of the alternative hypothesis: less than, not equal, or greater than.

NOTE: Remember the order that you input first and second samples has significance when you choose less than and greater than hypothesis alternatives.

7. Click **OK**

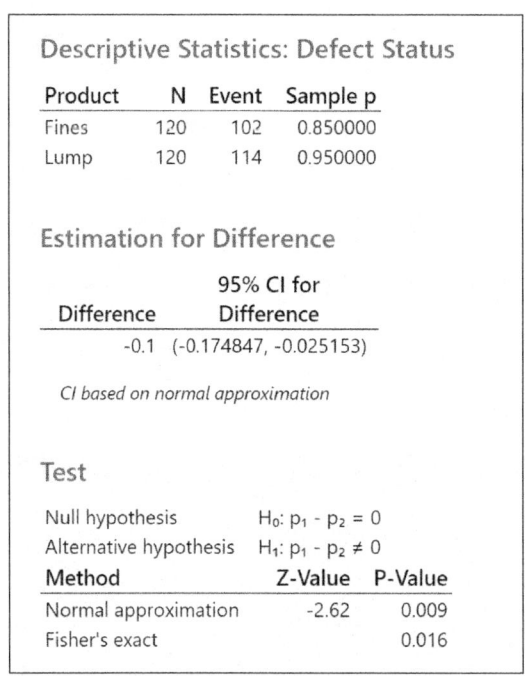

13.05 Test for Equal Variances

Used for checking for differences between variances – often an assumption for other statistical tests.

The Null and Alternative Hypothesis for the test might be:

H_0: Variances are equal
H_A: Not all variances are equal

Assumptions:

- Independent samples
- Normally distributed data (for the F test or Bartlett's test)
- Continuous probability distribution (for Levene's test)

The test - 2 SAMPLES ONLY:

1. Check data for normality (REFER TO NORMALITY TESTING)
2. Choose **Stat > Basic Statistics > 2 Variances**

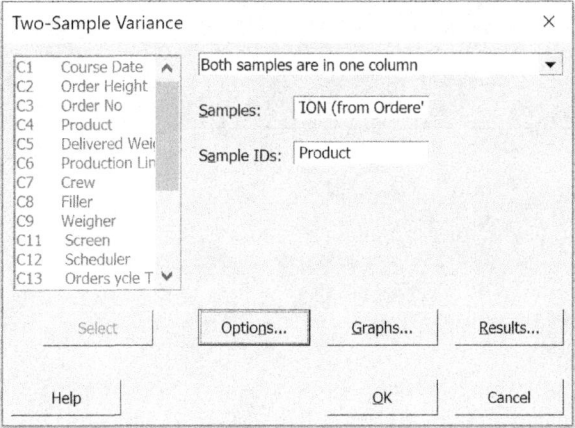

3. Select **Both samples are in one column** (stacked data), or whichever of the following reflects the data format:
   a. **Each sample is in its own column** (unstacked data), OR

b. **Sample standard deviations** (if you have standard deviation values for each sample), OR
c. **Sample variances** (if you have variance values for each sample)
4. **Samples:** (insert column containing the response variable)
5. **Sample IDs:** (insert column containing the categorical variable)
6. Select **Options**
7. **Check bottom box** if data is normally distributed
8. Click **OK** in all dialogue boxes

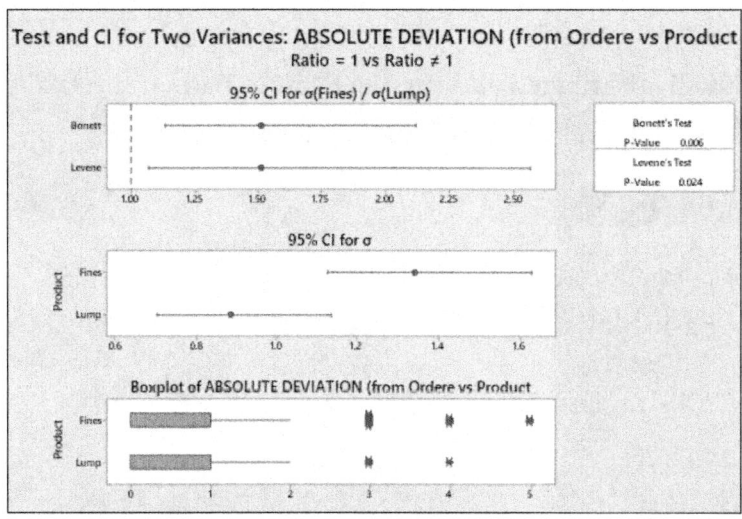

Descriptive Statistics

Product	N	StDev	Variance	95% CI for σ
Fines	120	1.345	1.809	(1.129, 1.629)
Lump	120	0.889	0.790	(0.705, 1.139)

Ratio of Standard Deviations

Estimated Ratio	95% CI for Ratio using Bonett	95% CI for Ratio using Levene
1.51368	(1.134, 2.122)	(1.072, 2.567)

Test

Null hypothesis: $H_0: \sigma_1 / \sigma_2 = 1$
Alternative hypothesis: $H_1: \sigma_1 / \sigma_2 \neq 1$
Significance level: $\alpha = 0.05$

Method	Test Statistic	DF1	DF2	P-Value
Bonett	7.67	1		0.006
Levene	5.13	1	238	0.024

The test – MORE THAN 2 SAMPLES: (Data must be stacked)

1. Check data for normality
2. Stack the data (if not already stacked)
3. Choose **Stat > ANOVA > Test for Equal Variances**

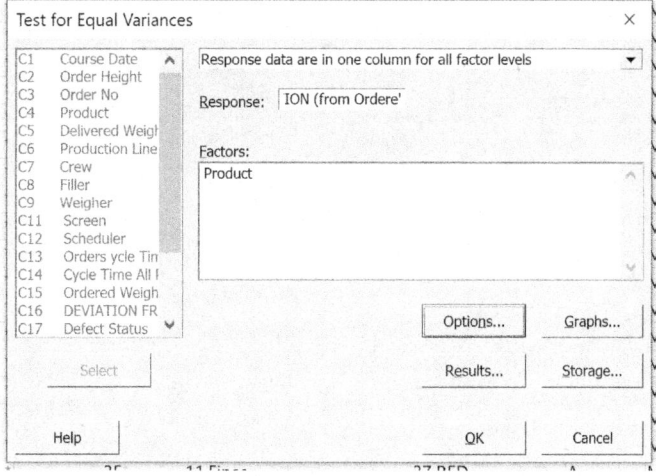

6. Choose **Response data are in one column for all factor levels** (one column of stacked data) or alternatively:
    a. **Response data are in a separate column for each factor level** (simply insert the separate columns containing the response data
4. **Response:** (insert the column containing the response variable)
5. **Factors:** (insert column that contains categorical variables in the model)
6. Select **Options**
7. Check the bottom box if data is **normally distributed** - (when checked, a parametric test will be used, if this is not checked, a non parametric test will be used)
8. Click **OK** in all dialogue boxes

The output for both normal and non normal data is shown on the following page.

The Non-Parametric - Levene's Test

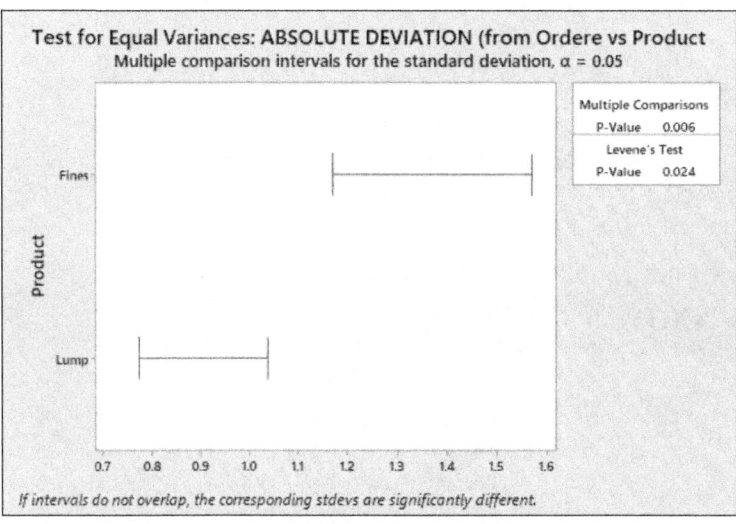

Levene's test is used for data from a continuous distribution that is **non-normal**

Parametric - F Test / Bartlett's Test

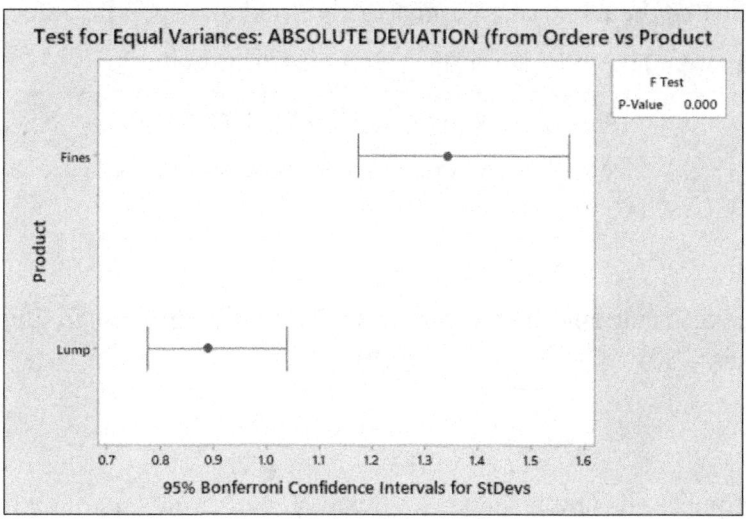

F-test (2 variances) or Bartlett's test (>2 variances) – used for **normal data**

13.06 1 Sample t-test

Tests the hypothesis that the mean of a population is equal to a specific value.

The Null and Alternative Hypothesis for the 1 Sample t-test might be:

> **H₀**: The mean is equal to the target value
> **Hₐ**: The mean is (< ≠ >) the target value

Assumptions:

- The distribution of sample means is Normally distributed (apply CLT for sample sizes ≥ 30)

The test:

1. Check for normality (if sample size is less than 30 data points *and* non normal use a non parametric test)
2. Choose **Stat > Basic Statistics > 1 Sample t**

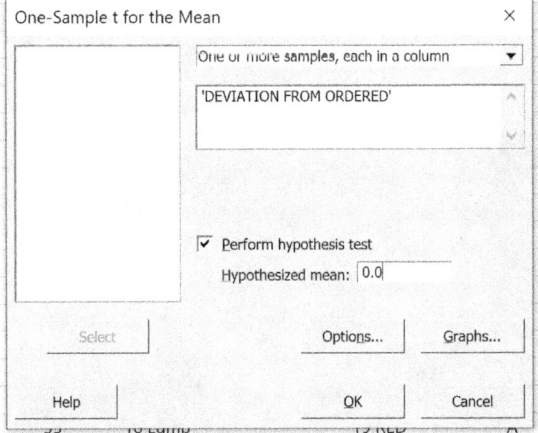

3. Select **One or more samples, each in a columns** (raw data is available), or **Summarised data** (sample statistics are known)
4. Check **Perform hypothesis test**
5. **Hypothesised mean:** (insert target value)
6. Select **Options**

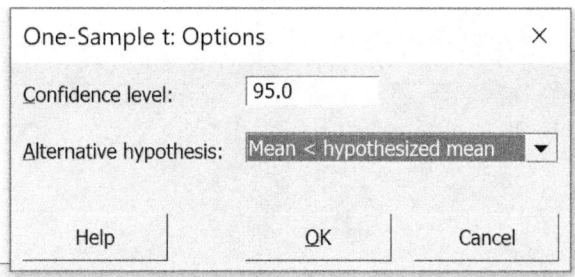

7. **Alternative hypothesis:** (select alternative hypothesis – less than / greater than / not equal)
8. Click **OK**
9. (optional) Select **Graphs**

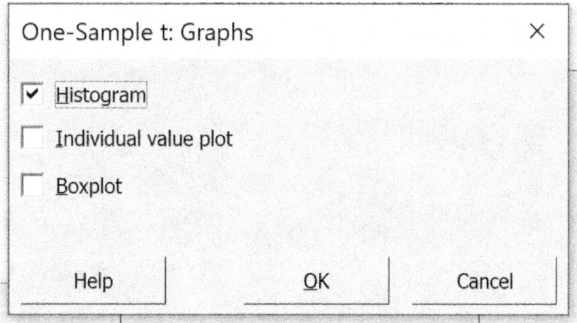

10. Check **Histogram**
11. Click **OK** in all dialogue boxes

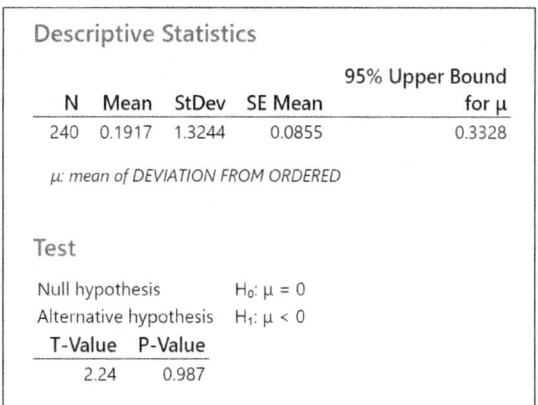

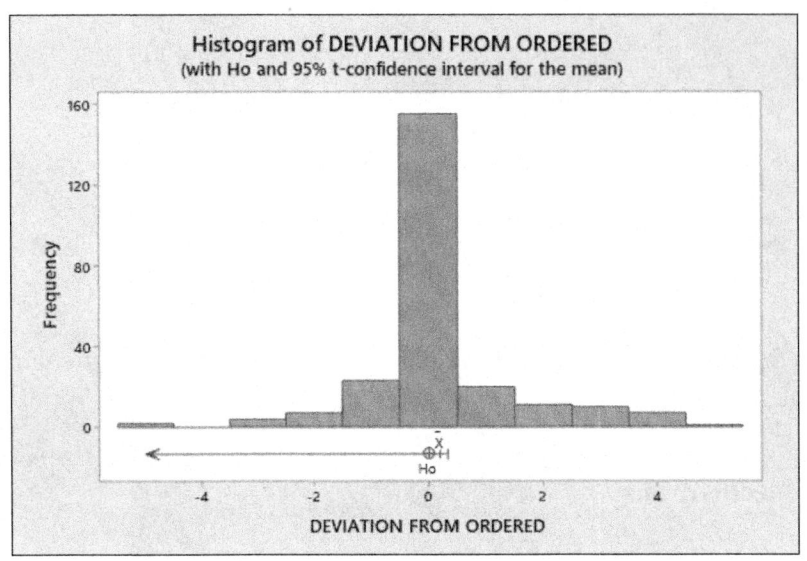

13.07 1 Sample Sign-test

This is a non-parametric test that tests the hypothesis that the median of a population is equal to a specific value.

The Null and Alternative Hypothesis for the 1 Sample Sign-test might be:

H_0: The median is equal to the target value
H_A: The median is (< ≠ >) the target value

Assumptions:

- Non normal data

The test:

1. Choose **Stat > Nonparametrics > 1 Sample Sign…**

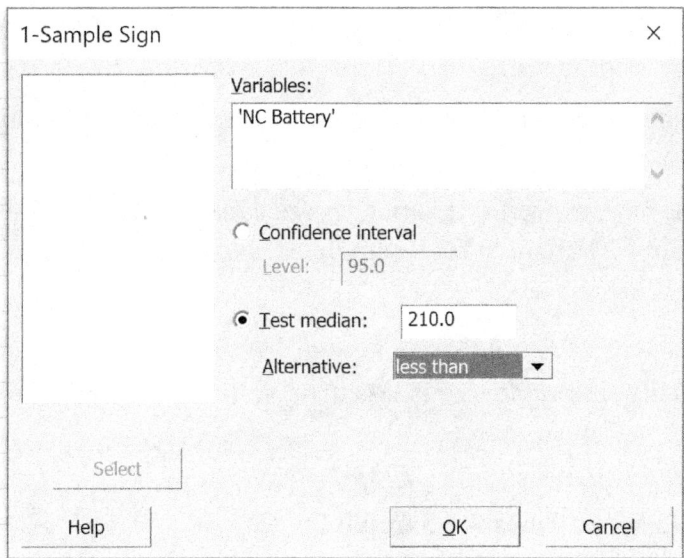

2. **Variables:** (insert columns containing the variables of interest)
3. Select **Test median** (to perform a sign-test – and specify the target median value)
4. Select the **Alternative:** hypothesis (from the choices select less than / greater than / not equal)
5. Click **OK** in all dialogue boxes

```
Test
Null hypothesis        H₀: η = 210
Alternative hypothesis H₁: η < 210
Sample        Number < 210  Number = 210  Number > 210  P-Value
NC Battery         13             0             12        0.500
```

13.08 2 Sample t-test

Used for checking for differences between means of two independent populations.

The Null and Alternative Hypothesis for the 2 Sample t-test might be:

> H_0: The mean of sample 1 = the mean of sample 2
>
> H_A: The mean of sample 1 is (< ≠ >) the mean of sample 2

Assumptions:

- Independent samples
- Distribution of sample means is Normally distributed (apply CLT for sample sizes ≥ 30)
- Test is more powerful if variances are equal (Test for Equal Variances for > 2 samples / 2 Variances for 2 samples)

The test:

1. Check for normality (if sample size is less than 30 data points *and* non normal use a non parametric test)
2. Test for equality of variances
3. Choose **Stat > Basic Statistics > 2 Sample t**

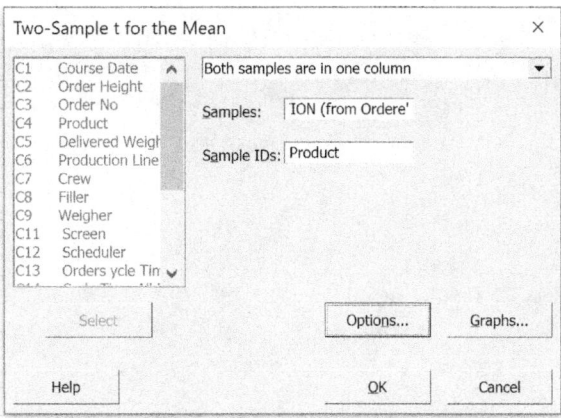

4. Select **Both samples are in one column** (stacked data), or alternatively:
    a. **Each sample is in its own column** (unstacked data), or
    b. **Summarised data** (sample size, mean and standard deviation of two data sets are known)
5. **Samples:** (insert the column containing the output data)
6. **Sample IDs:** (insert the column containing the categorical variable)
7. Select **Options**

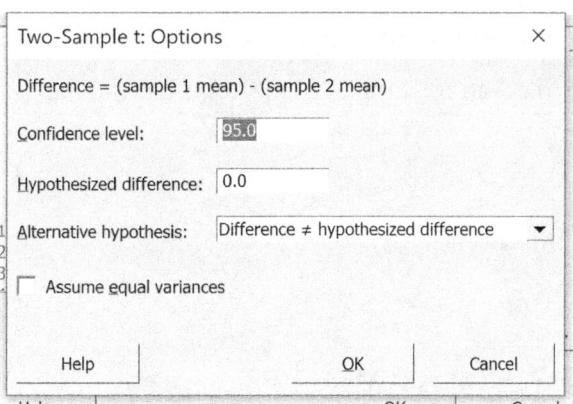

8. Select the **Alternative hypothesis:** (less than, greater than or non equal to)
9. Check **Assume equal variances:** (if they are equal)
10. **Alternative:** (select alternative hypothesis – less than / greater than / not equal)
11. Click **OK** in all dialogue boxes

```
Descriptive Statistics: ABSOLUTE DEVIATION (from Ordere

Product   N    Mean   StDev   SE Mean
Fines    120   0.85   1.35     0.12
Lump     120   0.517  0.889    0.081


Estimation for Difference

              95% CI for
Difference    Difference
   0.333     (0.043, 0.623)


Test

Null hypothesis         H₀: μ₁ - μ₂ = 0
Alternative hypothesis  H₁: μ₁ - μ₂ ≠ 0
T-Value   DF   P-Value
 2.27    206    0.025
```

13.09 Mann Whitney Test

Used for checking the location of two populations on the x-axis through comparison of medians.

The Null and Alternative Hypothesis for the Mann Whitney Test might be:

> H_0: The median of sample 1 = the median of sample 2
>
> H_A: The median of sample 1 is (< ≠ >) the median of sample 2

Assumptions:

- Independent samples

The test:

1. Choose **Stat > Nonparametrics > Mann-Whitney**

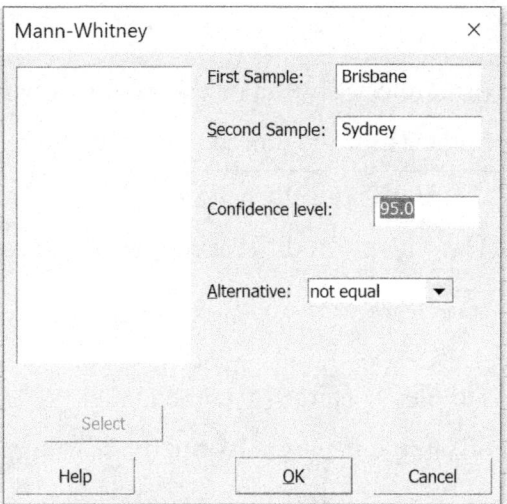

2. **First Sample:** (insert column containing first sample)
3. **Second Sample:** (insert column containing second sample)
4. **Alternative:** (select alternative hypothesis – less than / greater than / not equal)
5. Click **OK**

Descriptive Statistics

Sample	N	Median
Brisbane	20	1.540
Sydney	20	1.505

Estimation for Difference

Difference	CI for Difference	Achieved Confidence
0.235	(-0.6, 1)	95.01%

Test

Null hypothesis $H_0: \eta_1 - \eta_2 = 0$
Alternative hypothesis $H_1: \eta_1 - \eta_2 \neq 0$

Method	W-Value	P-Value
Not adjusted for ties	434.50	0.516
Adjusted for ties	434.50	0.516

13.10 Paired t-test

Used for checking the mean difference between paired populations.

The Null and Alternative Hypothesis for the Paired t-test might be:

> H_0: The mean difference = zero
>
> H_A: The mean difference is ($< \neq >$) zero

Assumptions:

- Data from 2 samples is paired by some factor
- Distribution of sample means is Normally distributed (apply CLT for sample sizes ≥ 30)

The test:

1. Test for **normality** (and if less than 30 data points that are non-normally distributed, use a non parametric alternative)
2. Choose **Stat > Basic Statistics > Paired t**
3. Select **Each samples is in a column** (unstacked data), or alternatively:
   a. **Summarised data (differences)** (sample size, mean and standard deviation of the difference between the two data sets is known)

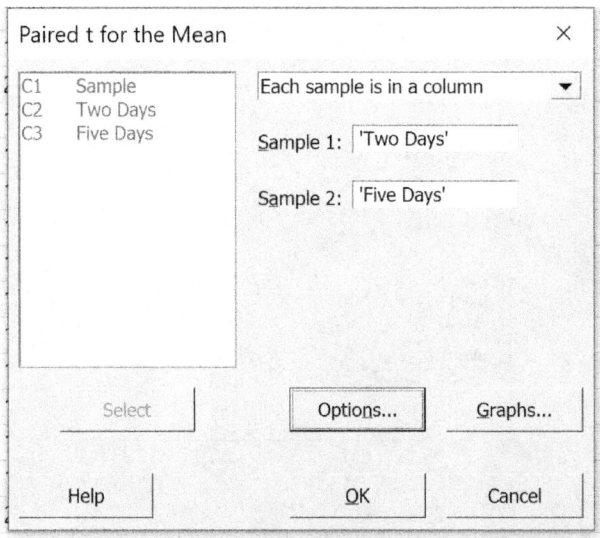

4. **Sample 1:** (insert the column containing the first sample)
5. **Sample 2:** (insert the column containing the second sample)
6. Select **Options**

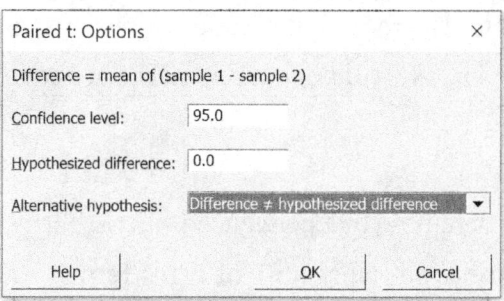

7. **Alternative:** (select alternative hypothesis – less than / greater than / not equal)
8. Click **OK** in all dialogue boxes

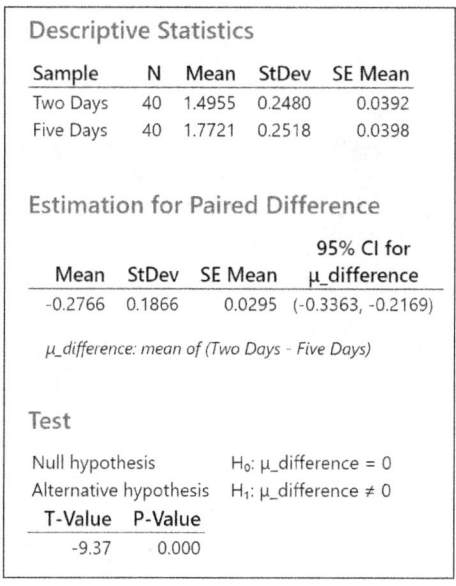

13.11 One Way ANOVA

Used for checking for differences between means of 3 or more independent populations.

The Null and Alternative Hypothesis for the 1 Way ANOVA test might be:

> H_0: The means of all populations are equal
>
> H_A: Not all population means are equal

Assumptions:

- Independent samples (Independence of Error Terms)
- Normal Distribution (Normality of Error Terms) NOTE - slight departures from normality are not a cause for concern
- Equal Variances (Constant Variance of Error Terms)

The test: (STACKED DATA)

1. Choose **Stat > ANOVA > One-Way**

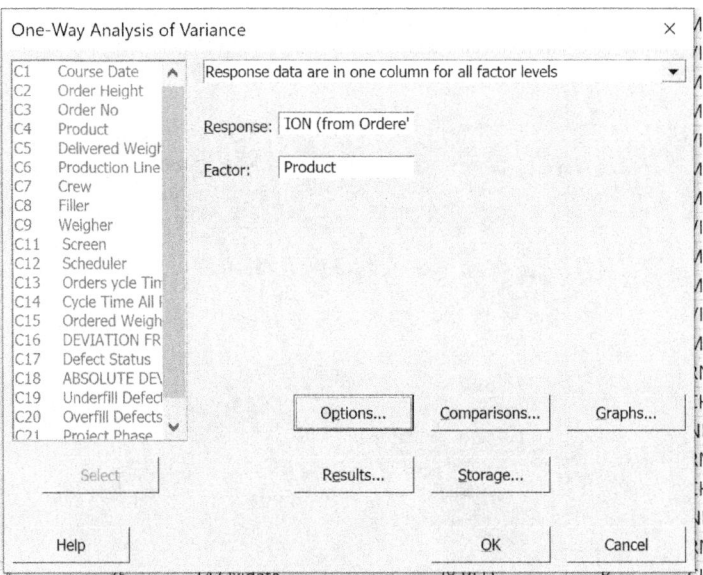

2. Select **Response data are in one column for all factor levels** (stacked data)
3. **Response:** (insert column containing the response variable)

4. **Factor:** (insert column that contains the relevant factor levels / categorical variable)
5. Select **Options**

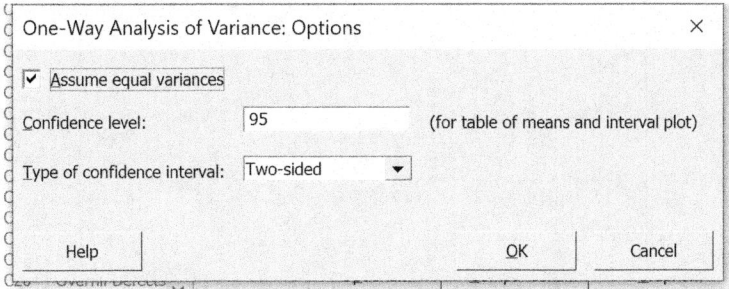

6. Check **Assume Equal Variances** if they are the same
7. Click **OK**
8. Select **Graphs**

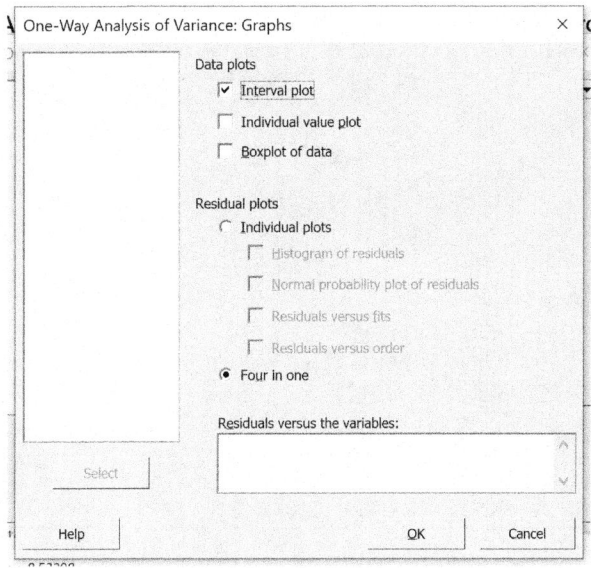

9. **Residual Plots:** check **Four in one**
10. Click **OK** in all dialogue boxes

Analysis of Variance

Source	DF	Adj SS	Adj MS	F-Value	P-Value
Product	2	157.9	78.96	1.08	0.339
Error	357	25999.9	72.83		
Total	359	26157.8			

Model Summary

S	R-sq	R-sq(adj)	R-sq(pred)
8.53398	0.60%	0.05%	0.00%

Means

Product	N	Mean	StDev	95% CI
Fines	120	0.850	1.345	(-0.682, 2.382)
Lump	120	0.5167	0.8886	(-1.0154, 2.0488)
Oxidate	120	2.06	14.69	(0.53, 3.59)

Pooled StDev = 8.53398

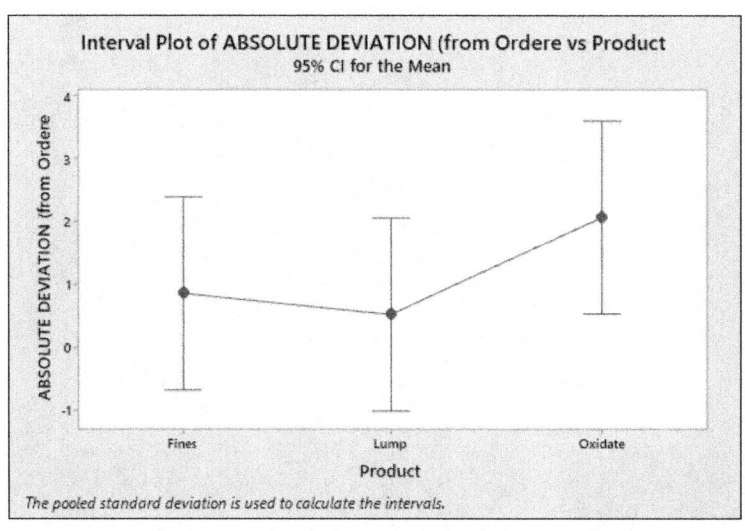

The test: (UNSTACKED DATA)

1. Choose **Stat > ANOVA > One-Way**
2. Select **Response data are in a separate column for each factor level** (unstacked data)
3. **Responses:** (insert columns containing the response variables)
4. Select **Options**
5. Check **Assume Equal Variances** if they are the same
6. Click **OK**
7. Select **Graphs**
8. **Residual Plots:** check **Three in one**
9. Click **OK** in all dialogue boxes

Check Validity of ANOVA using Residuals

The validity of any ANOVA study is determined by a study of residuals. The assumptions associated with the model are:

Normality of Error: Error values should be normally distributed with a mean of zero.

NORMAL PROBABILITY PLOT – should be close to a straight line.

Constant Error Variance: The variance of error values does not change for different levels of a factor or according to the values of the predicted response.

RESIDUALS VERSUS THE FITTED VALUES PLOT – variation remains constant for all fitted values.

Independence of Error: Each error value (residual) is independent of all other errors.

RESIDUALS VERSUS THE ORDER OF THE DATA – no obvious patterns indicating a time related effect.

Note: This chart does not appear when you are using data laid out in separate columns and choose the **Three in one** residuals plot.

MINITAB STATISTICAL ANALYSIS HANDBOOK - VERSION 21

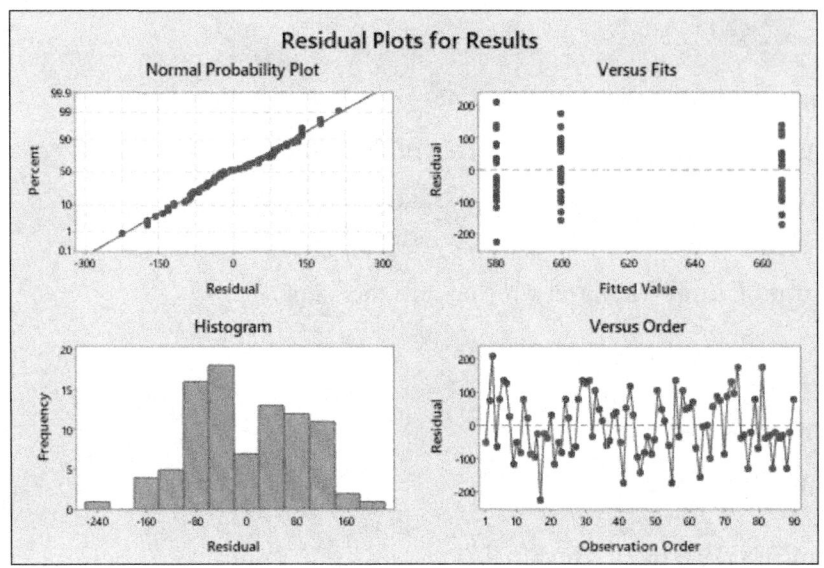

13.12 Mood's Median Test

Used for checking for differences between medians of 3 or more independent populations.
The Null and Alternative Hypothesis for the 1 Way ANOVA test might be:

> H_0: The medians of all populations are equal
> H_A: Not all population medians are equal

Assumptions:

- Independent samples
- Similar distribution shapes
- Equal variances

The test (Data must be stacked):

1. Test equality of variances
2. Test distribution shapes (generate individual histograms or box plots)
3. Choose **Stat > Nonparametrics > Mood's Median Test**

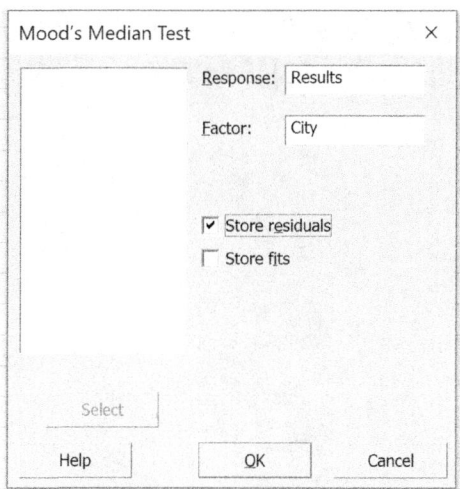

4. **Response:** (insert column containing the response variable)
5. **Factor:** (insert column that contains the relevant factor levels)
6. **Store residuals:** (check if you intend to study residuals)

7. **Store fits:** (check if you want to study residuals versus fits)
8. Click **OK**

Descriptive Statistics

City	Median	N <= Overall Median	N > Overall Median	Q3 – Q1	95% Median CI
Brisbane	557	18	12	165.00	(517.431, 647.937)
Melbourne	581	19	11	147.25	(561, 669.027)
Sydney	679	8	22	115.00	(620.915, 717)
Overall	605				

Test

Null hypothesis H_0: The population medians are all equal
Alternative hypothesis H_1: The population medians are not all equal

DF	Chi-Square	P-Value
2	9.87	0.007

Checking Validity With Residuals

Whilst constant variance assumption can be assessed statistically by undertaking a test for equal variances, the assumption can be visually assessed by generating a scatter plot of residuals (Y) versus fits (X).

When the error variance does not change for different levels of a factor or according to the values of the predicted response, the data sets exhibit constant variance.

RESIDUALS VERSUS THE FITTED VALUES PLOT – variation remains constant for all fitted values.

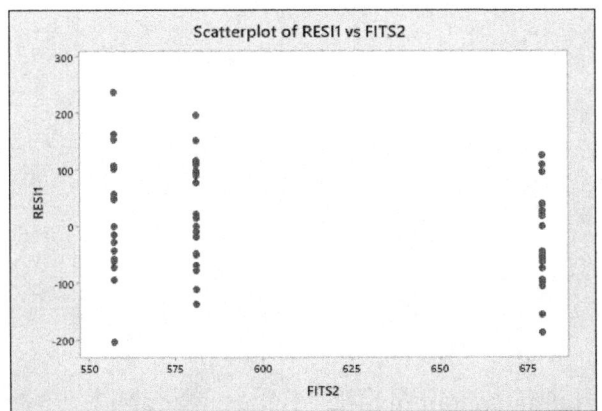

14. HYPOTHESIS TESTING APPLICATION EXAMPLES

14.01 Hypothesis Testing – General Application

Chi-Square

Safety - Comparing proportions of work injuries by type (hand, eye, body, other) with other mine sites – to determine if the proportion of hand injuries was the same or different.

Staffing – Comparing the proportion of male and female employees between different organisations.

Competency – Studying the proportion of defects in processing applications, for before and after training to make a determination about the value of the training being given.

Industrial – To understand if a business has proportionately, more or less working days lost through industrial action than other businesses.

Proportion of Defects – Comparing before and after scenarios to determine if the proportion of defects after improvement is less than it was before the improvement work was undertaken.

1 Sample t-test

Air Emissions – the air emissions from a plant was compared to the maximum value stated in the license to operate to determine if they were conforming.

Production – testing to see if the average diameter of a manufactured part is the same as the customers' specification.

2 Sample t-test

Phone Repair Times – testing to see if the average time taken to repair phones with cameras took longer than time to repair phones without cameras.

Production Lines – the mean yield (% recoveries) for each flotation circuit was compared to determine if there was a different between the two, it was suspected that one was performing less than the other

Shovel Output – An Australian mining company compared the output of their shovels to the output of shovels operating at a similar mine in North America

Shift Output – testing to see if the day shift and night shift production outputs differ.

Before and After – Comparing before and after scenarios to determine if averages after improvement are less than before improvement.

Paired t-test

Tyres – a mine ran a mileage test on two different tyre types, differences in results were confirmed by comparing the mean mileages of each – these were paired by truck (a tyre from each supplier was put on the front and rear of each test truck)

Golf Ball Distance – a golfing company provides 25 golfers with two different types of balls to test driving distances, the mean distance of each brand golf ball was compared to the other – these were paired by golfer.

Test for Equal Variances

Production Lines – A test was conducted between two flotation circuits to see if the variance of each was the same or different. It was suspected that one had greater variation than the other.

Tensile Strength – a manufacturing plant tested to see if the variation in tensile strength for a manufactured part differed between seasons. It was suspected that during colder months, tensile strength varied to a greater level resulting in more breakages.

1 Way ANOVA

Load Times – the mean rail loading times for ore was compared for five different mine sites to determine if there was statistically significant difference between them. Once confirmed, the site with the best performance was benchmarked so that leading practices could be shared amongst the other four.

Seed Life – the useful life of seeds was evaluated under 4 different temperature settings. The results obtained from all temperature settings were compared to determine if there was in fact a difference.

14.02 Hypothesis Testing – Six Sigma Projects

Chi-Square

Reduce lost working days – To understand if a department has proportionately, more or less working days lost through injury than other departments. The team working on reducing leave due to injury can identify the source of greatest loss.

Reducing connection delays due to addressing faults – A team compared the proportion of address faults by category amongst different geographical regions to find the area with the most defects associated with one specific category.

1 Sample t-test

Production – testing to see if the average diameter of a manufactured part is the same as the customers' specification.

2 Sample t-test

Reduce cycle time – The average cycle time of week days and weekends were compared to find out if either was a source of excess cycle time.

Shift Output – testing to see if the day shift and night shift production outputs differ.

Reduce repair cycle time – A comparison between average cycle time for repair of mobile phones before improvement and after was conducted to support the hypothesis that improvements had in fact been achieved.

Paired t-test

Resin Strength – Resin was poured into 20 different moulds at a boat manufacturing facility. The strength of the resin in each mould was measured after 2 days of curing and after 5 days of curing to study if shorter curing time reduced strength. Each 2 day and 5 day value is paired according to the mould they were taken from.

Tyres – Conducting a mileage test on two different tyre types, differences in results were confirmed by comparing the mean mileages of each – these were paired by truck (a tyre from each supplier was put on the front and rear of each test truck)

Test for Equal Variances

Reduce cycle time variation – A test was conducted to see if the variation in cycle time for delivering ordered parts each day of the week was the same.

Reducing Breakages – a team in a manufacturing plant tested to see if the variation in tensile strength for a manufactured part differed between materials supplied by different suppliers. It was suspected that tensile strength varied to a greater level from one supplier resulting in more breakages and the test was used to validate root cause analysis.

1 Way ANOVA

Reduce PC Deployment Time – A team in an IT department of a major corporation compared the mean delivery times for deployment of different types of PC's (laptops, desktops, servers) to determine if there was a difference. The goal was to find the source of the most cycle time.

15. CORRELATION ANALYSIS

15.01 Correlation versus Regression

CORRELATION is the study of relationships between variables with the goal of understanding if movement of one variable causes a corresponding movement in another variable.

REGRESSION is the creation of models for the purpose of predicting the response in one variable when another variable is changed.

15.02 The Process

A correlation study is conducted according to the following sequence.

Understand Correlation (the Relationship between Variables)

The purpose of this is to establish the strength of cause and effect relationships. This would be the only step we use if cause and effect analysis was our only requirement. We use this in the analyse phase of the DMAIC sequence.

    Step 1. Construct and Analyse Plots

    Step 2. Measure Correlation

Develop a Regression Model (for predicting and optimising input variables)

We would use this step only if we were going to develop a prediction model for the purpose of defining settings for some specific output. We would use this in the solution phase of the DMAIC sequence.

    Step 3. Develop the Regression Model

    Step 4. Validate the Regression Model

15.03 Visual Correlation Analysis

Generate Scatter Plots

The basic option is to visually determine the strength of the relationship between a potential cause and the effect using a scatter plot.

1. Choose **Graph > Scatterplot**

2. Select **Simple** type of scatterplot from the graph gallery: (or for certain situations choose with groups, with regression etc)

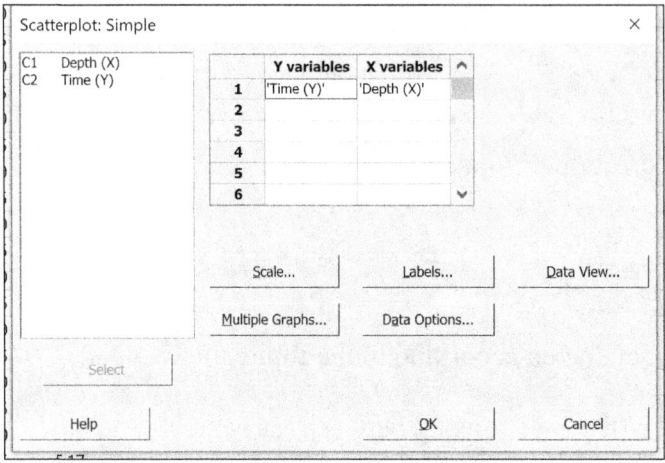

3. **Y variables:** (insert column containing dependent variable)
4. **X variables:** (insert column containing independent variable)
5. Click **OK**

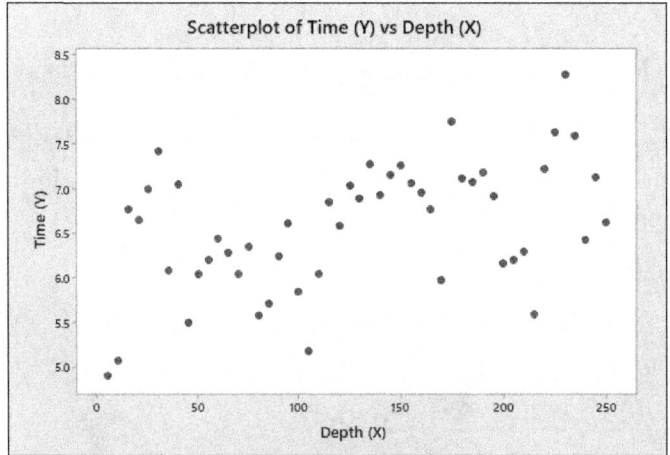

Generate Fitted Line Plot

You can also use a fitted line plot for plotting a single Y and it's relationship with a single X.

1. Choose **Stat > Regression > Fitted Line Plot**

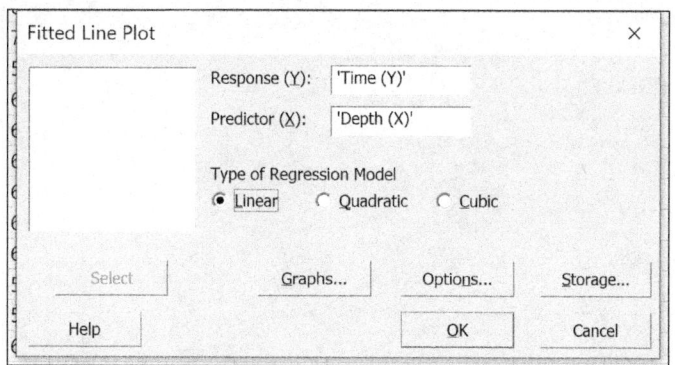

2. **Response (Y):** (insert column containing dependent variable)
3. **Predictor (X):** (insert column containing independent variable)
4. Check **OK**

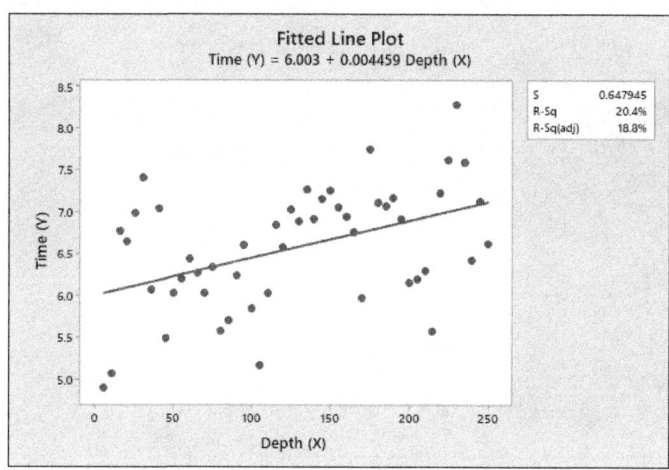

Fitted Line Plot – With Confidence Bands:

1. Choose **Stat > Regression > Fitted Line Plot**
2. **Response (Y):** (insert column containing dependent variable)
3. **Predictor (X):** (insert column containing independent variable)
4. Select **Options**

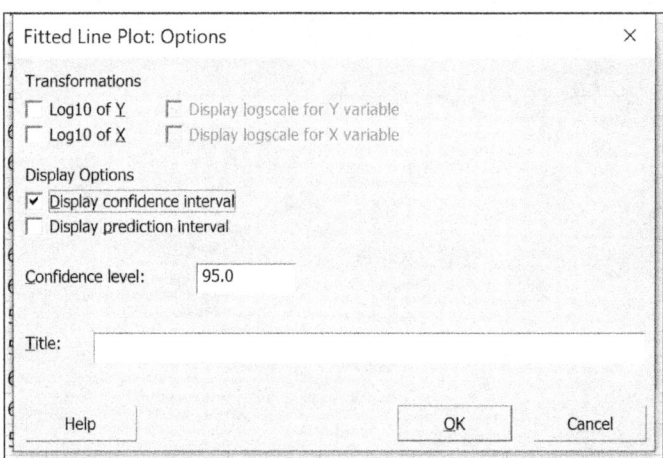

5. Check **Display confidence interval** to display confidence bands about the fitted regression line at the level of confidence specified
6. Click **OK** in all dialogue boxes

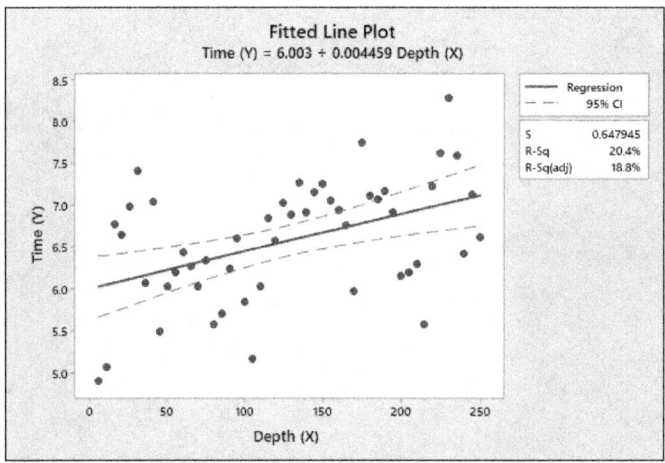

Generating Matrix Plots

As an alternative to scatter plots, matrix plots can be used to visually determine the strength of the relationship between more than one potential cause and the effect on a single chart.

1. Choose **Graph > Matrix Plot**
2. Choose **'Simple'** from the graph gallery and Click **OK**

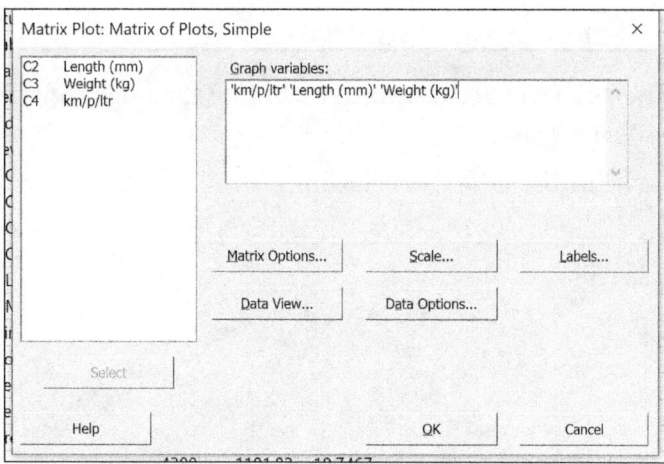

3. **Graph variables:** (insert all columns containing the Y and all X variables in your study)
4. (Optional) Select **Matrix Options** and then choose the correct **Matrix Display:** (select lower left or upper right – displays one chart of all combinations)
5. Click **OK** in all dialogue boxes

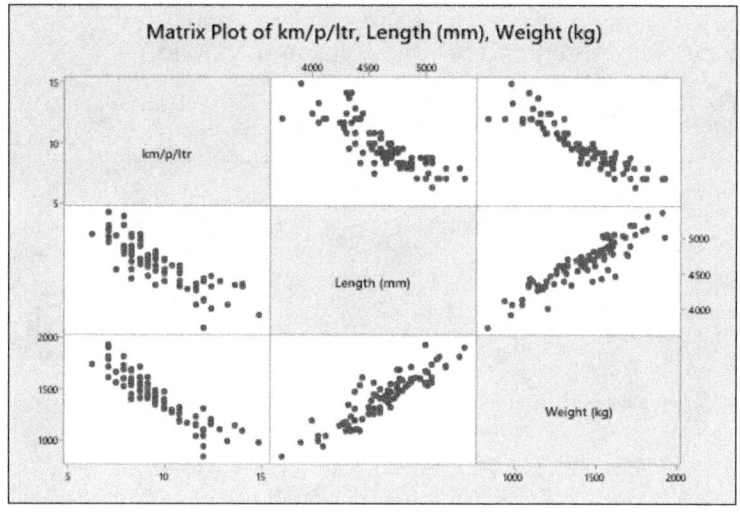

15.04 Compute Correlation (Includes Matrix Plot)

The 'Correlation Coefficient' (R) measures the strength of the linear relationship between dependent and independent variables.

1. Choose **Stat > Basic Statistics > Correlation**

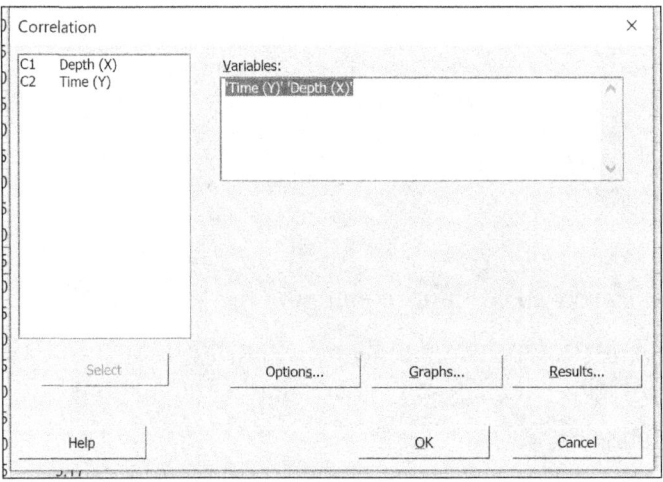

2. **Variables:** (insert columns containing variables in the model)
3. Select **Options**

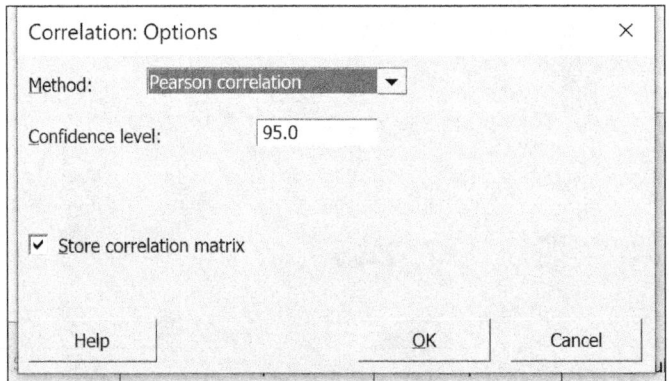

4. Check **Store correlation matrix**
5. Click **OK**
6. Select **Graphs**

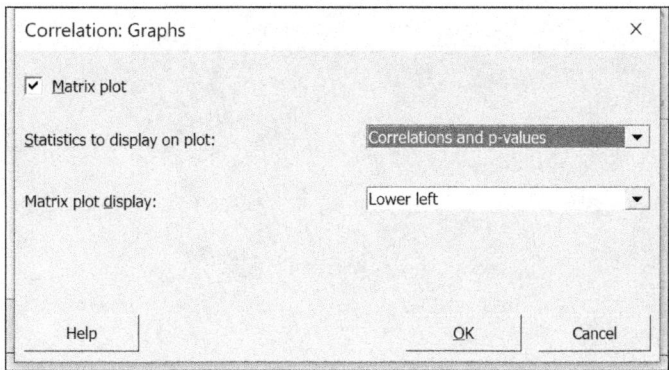

7. **Statistics to display on plot:** choose Correlations and P-values
8. Click **OK**
9. Select **Results**

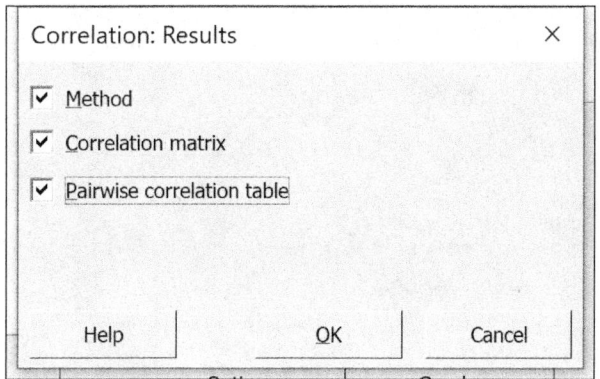

10. Check **Pairwise correlation table**
11. Click **OK** in all dialogue boxes

MINITAB STATISTICAL ANALYSIS HANDBOOK - VERSION 21

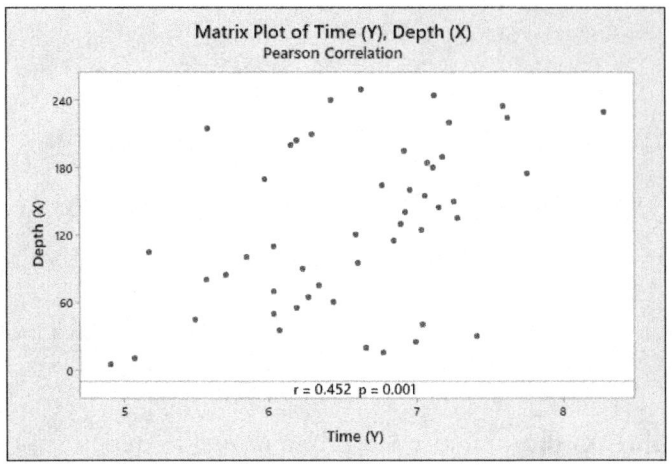

R Values:

    a. **R = -1.00:** Perfectly negative linear relationship

    b. **R = 1.00:** Perfectly positive linear relationship

    c. **R = 0.00:** No linear relationship

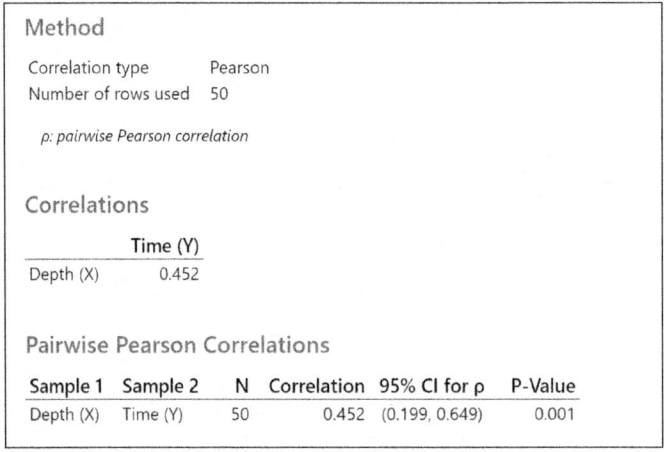

P-Values: The P-value is used to make a decision as to whether or not correlation coefficients are statistically significant (ie; $R \neq 0$).

When the P-value is less than α (usually 0.05), the correlation coefficient (R) is statistically significant.

15.05 Summary of Terms – Correlation

R

Definition - Correlation Coefficient

Range of Values - -1 to +1

Meaning - An indication of the strength of the linear relationship between the response (Y values) and the independent variable (X values). A result close to zero indicates no relationship.

R^2 - R-sq and R-sq (adjusted)

Definition - Coefficient of Determination

Range of Values - 0.00 to 1.00

Meaning - R-sq indicates the amount of variation in the response (Y values) that is explained by its relationship with the independent variable (X values). Multiply by 100 to explain the relationship by %. A modified R-sq is *adjusted* for the number of terms in the model. When unnecessary terms are included in the model, R-sq can be artificially high.

P-Value (for Correlation Coefficient)

Definition - The probability that the slope is significantly different than zero

Range of Values - 0.00 to 1.00

Meaning - If the P-value is less than 0.05, the correlation coefficient R is significant. It indicates there is a significant correlation between variables.

16. REGRESSION MODELLING

16.01 Correlation versus Regression

CORRELATION is the study of relationships between variables with the goal of understanding if movement of one variable causes a corresponding movement in another variable.

REGRESSION is the creation of models for the purpose of predicting the response in one variable when another variable is changed.

16.02 The Process

A correlation and regression study is conducted according to the following sequence.

Understand Correlation (the Relationship between Variables)

The purpose of this is to establish the strength of cause and effect relationships. This would be the only step we use if cause and effect analysis was our only requirement. We use this in the analyse phase of the DMAIC sequence.

    Step 1. Construct and Analyse Plots

    Step 2. Measure Correlation

Refer to the Section titled 'Correlation' for instructions on how to complete this.

Develop a Regression Model (for predicting and optimising input variables)

We would use this step only if we were going to develop a prediction model for the purpose of defining settings for some specific output. We would use this in the solution phase of the DMAIC sequence.

    Step 3. Develop the Regression Model

    Step 4. Validate the Regression Model

16.03 Developing a Simple Regression Model

1. Choose **Stat >Regression > Regression >Fit Regression Model**

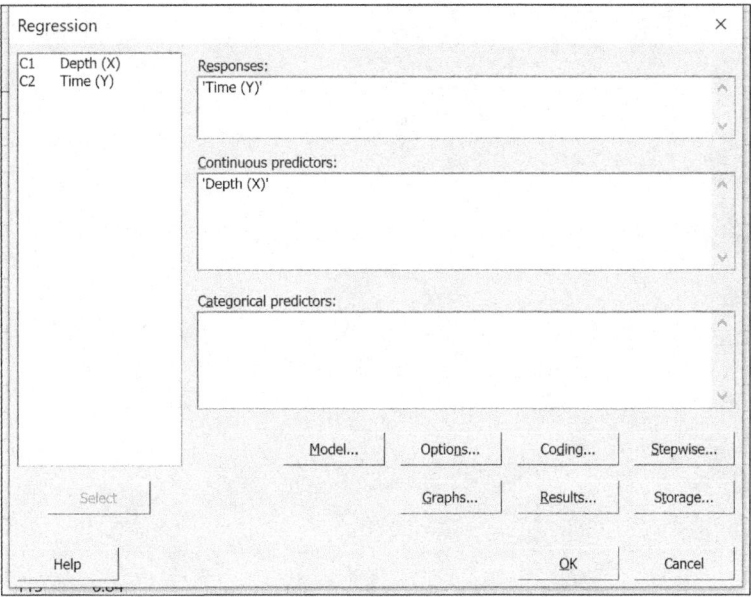

2. **Response:** (insert column containing the dependent variable)
3. **Continuous predictors:** (insert column containing the independent numerical variables)
4. **Categorical predictors:** (insert column containing the independent categorical variables)
5. Select **Graphs**

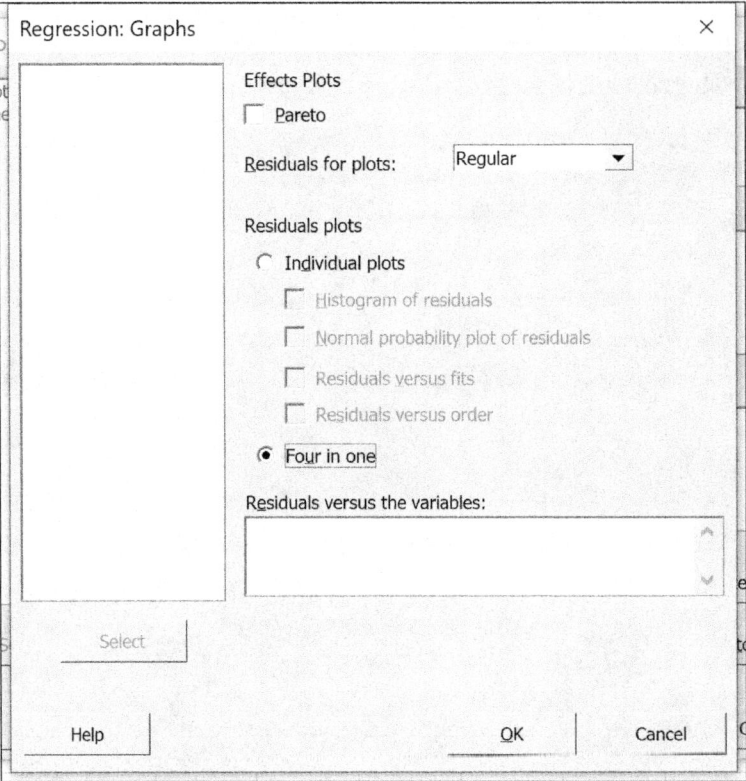

6. **Residual Plots:** select **Four in one**
7. Click **OK** in all dialogue boxes

Regression Analysis: Time (Y) versus Depth (X)

Coefficients

Term	Coef	SE Coef	T-Value	P-Value	VIF
Constant	6.003	0.186	32.26	0.000	
Depth (X)	0.00446	0.00127	3.51	0.001	1.00

Model Summary

S	R-sq	R-sq(adj)	R-sq(pred)
0.647945	20.43%	18.78%	12.35%

Analysis of Variance

Source	DF	Adj SS	Adj MS	F-Value	P-Value
Regression	1	5.176	5.1756	12.33	0.001
Depth (X)	1	5.176	5.1756	12.33	0.001
Error	48	20.152	0.4198		
Total	49	25.328			

R-Sq: The 'Coefficient of Determination' (R^2) measures the percentage of variation in Y explained by the linear relationship of X and Y

P-Values: The P-value is used to make a decision as to whether or not coefficients are statistically significant (ie; $R^2 \neq 0$). When the P-value is less than α (usually 0.05), the coefficient is statistically significant.

16.04 Check Validity Of The Regression Model

The validity of any regression study is determined by a study of residuals. The assumptions associated with the regression are:

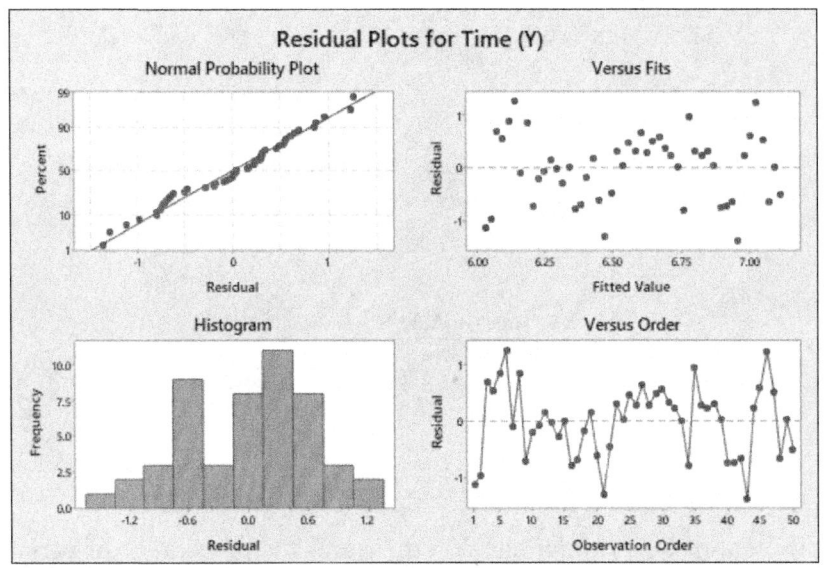

Normality of Error:

Errors around the line of regression (residuals) should be normally distributed with a mean of zero. NORMAL PROBABILITY PLOT – should be close to a straight line.

Constant Variance:

The variation around the line of regression should be constant for all values of x. RESIDUALS VERSUS THE FITTED VALUES PLOT – variation remains constant for all fitted values.

Independence of Errors:

Errors (residuals) should be independent for all values of x. RESIDUALS VERSUS THE ORDER OF THE DATA – no obvious patterns indicating a time related effect.

16.05 Developing a Multiple Linear Regression Model

Use to determine relationships between multiple X's and a Y.

1. Choose **Stat >Regression > Regression > Fit Regression Model**

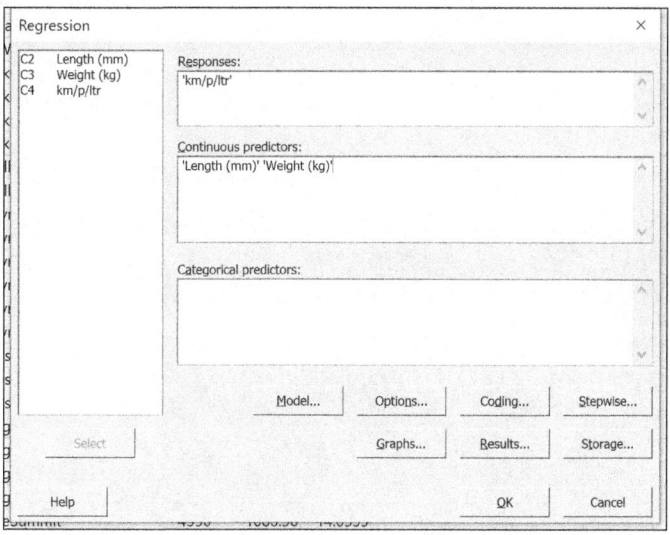

2. **Responses:** (insert columns containing the dependent (Y) variables)
3. **Continuous predictors:** (insert columns containing the independent numerical variables)
4. **Categorical predictors:** (insert columns containing the independent categorical variables)
5. Select **Graphs**

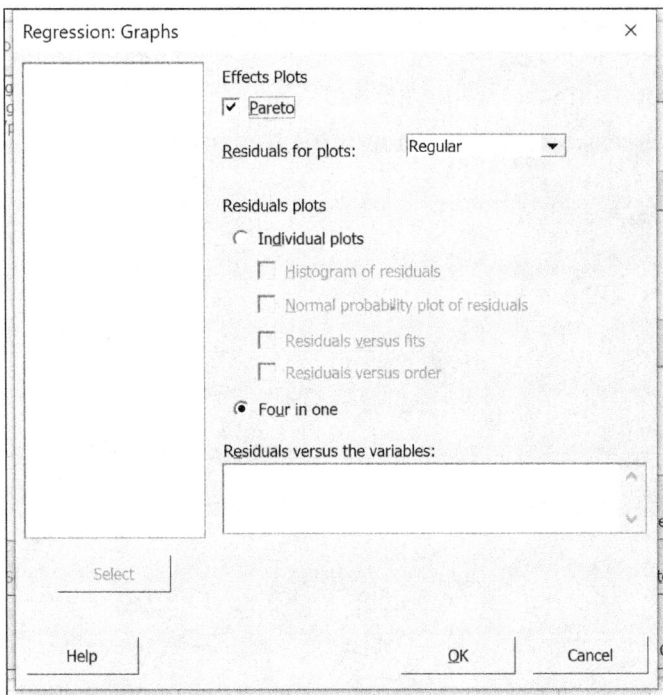

6. **Effects Plots:** Check **Pareto**
7. **Residual Plots:** Check **Four in one**
8. Click **OK** in all dialogue boxes

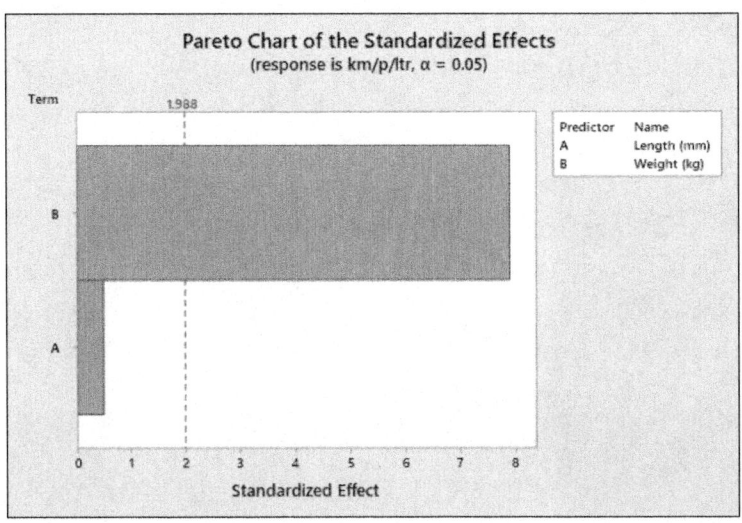

Pareto Chart of Effects: displays the effect of each predictor variable against a P-value (red line), those variables that cross to the right are significant in the model, those that do not cross are insignificant.

```
Coefficients

Term            Coef      SE Coef    T-Value   P-Value   VIF
Constant        20.67     1.81       11.41     0.000
Length (mm)    -0.000310  0.000611   -0.51     0.613     5.63
Weight (kg)    -0.006748  0.000855   -7.90     0.000     5.63


Model Summary

     S       R-sq    R-sq(adj)   R-sq(pred)
  0.803365   82.05%    81.64%      80.33%


Analysis of Variance

Source        DF    Adj SS    Adj MS   F-Value   P-Value
Regression     2    253.793   126.896  196.62    0.000
  Length (mm)  1      0.166     0.166    0.26    0.613
  Weight (kg)  1     40.231    40.231   62.34    0.000
Error         86     55.504     0.645
  Lack-of-Fit 79     54.735     0.693    6.31    0.008
  Pure Error   7      0.769     0.110
Total         88    309.297
```

VIF: (Variance Inflation Factors) is a measure of co-linearity between predictors (X's). (if the X's are uncorrelated VIF = 1; if VIF is > 5, regression coefficients may be poorly estimated and at least one of the terms must be dropped from the model)

R-Sq: The 'Coefficient of Determination' (R^2) measures the percentage of variation in Y explained by the linear relationship of X's and Y

Adjusted R Square: This is a modified measure of (R^2) that takes into consideration the number of terms and number of data points in the model. As the number of terms increases in the model (multiple linear regression), this value will get smaller when these terms offer little value to the regression.

P-Values: The P-value is used to make a decision as to whether or not coefficients are statistically significant (ie; $R^2 \neq 0$). When the P-value is less than α (usually 0.05), the coefficient is statistically significant.

16.06 Check Validity Of The Regression Model

The validity of any regression study is determined by a study of residuals. The assumptions associated with the regression are:

Normality of Error:

Errors around the line of regression (residuals) should be normally distributed with a mean of zero. NORMAL PROBABILITY PLOT – should be close to a straight line.

Constant Variance:

The variation around the line of regression should be constant for all values of x. RESIDUALS VERSUS THE FITTED VALUES PLOT – variation remains constant for all fitted values.

Independence of Errors:

Errors (residuals) should be independent for all values of x. RESIDUALS VERSUS THE ORDER OF THE DATA – no obvious patterns indicating a time related effect.

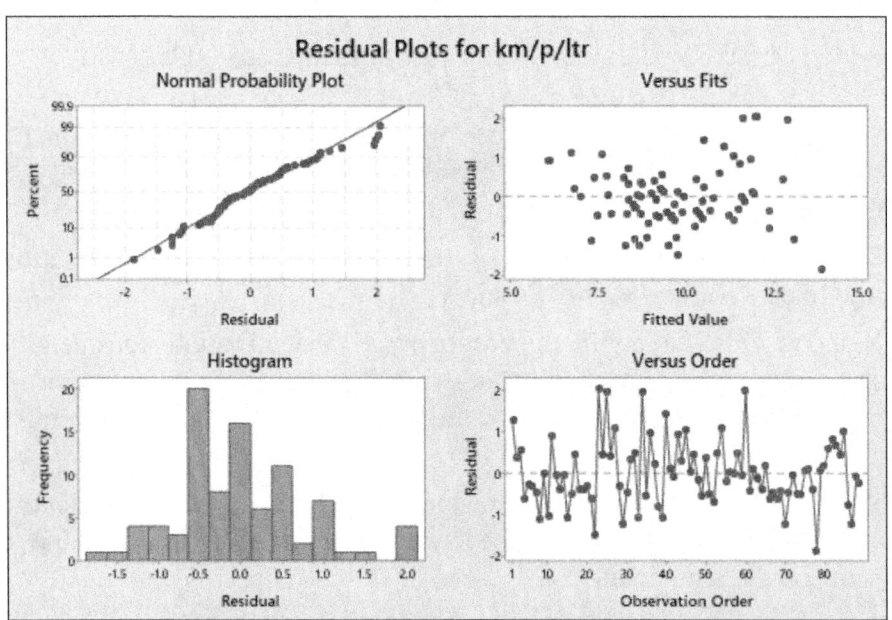

16.07 Summary of Terms – Linear Regression

R

Definition - Correlation Coefficient

Range of Values - -1 to +1

Meaning - An indication of the strength of the linear relationship between the response (Y values) and the independent variable (X values). A result close to zero indicates no relationship.

R^2 - R-sq and R-sq (adjusted)

Definition - Coefficient of Determination

Range of Values - 0.00 to 1.00

Meaning - R-sq indicates the amount of variation in the response (Y values) that is explained by its relationship with the independent variable (X values). Multiply by 100 to explain the relationship by %. A modified R-sq is *adjusted* for the number of terms in the model. When unnecessary terms are included in the model, R-sq can be artificially high.

P-Value (for Regression Model)

Definition - The probability that the slope is significantly different than zero

Range of Values - 0.00 to 1.00

Meaning - If the P-value is less than 0.05, the slope of the fitted line is significantly different than zero, and there is a linear relationship between the response (Y values) and the independent variable (X values)

Residual

Definition - The difference between an observed value of Y and the predicted value of Y

Range of Values - No Limit

Meaning - Where common cause variation exists only, residuals will be normally distributed with a mean of zero.

S

<u>Definition</u> - Standard deviation of residuals

<u>Range of Values</u> - 0 and higher

<u>Meaning</u> - This gives an indication of how much the typical observed value differs from the predicted value.

Standardised Residual

<u>Definition</u> - Equals the residual divided by the standard deviation

<u>Range of Values</u> - -3 to +3 (approximately)

<u>Meaning</u> - A standardised residual with an absolute value of >3 is an unusual observation that should be investigated.

Influential Observation

<u>Definition</u> - An observation with an X value that has a large influence on the values of coefficients.

<u>Range of Values</u> - No limit

<u>Meaning</u> - Can be observed as an outlier. A decision is necessary as to whether they should be included in the regression analysis.

VIF

<u>Definition</u> - Variance Inflation Factor

<u>Range of Values</u> - 1 and higher

<u>Meaning</u> - A measure of collinearity between predictor variables. Results above 5 may indicate that there is excessive correlation between predictor variables, hence regression coefficients may be poorly estimated.

As Xs are controlled independently of others, you will see a VIF of 1 in the regression table.

17. TWO WAY ANOVA / BALANCED ANOVA

TYPE OF DESIGN	NUMBER OF X's	USED WHEN WANT TO IDENTIFY -
2 FACTOR FACTORIAL (2 Way ANOVA)	2	All main effects and interactions

17.01 Experimental Design Process

A Two Way ANOVA is conducted according to the following process.

Step 1 – Identify the response, factors and factor levels

- Two factors
- Multiple level settings

Step 2 – Select type of design

- With replication
- Without replication

Step 3 – Run experiment

- Insert data into worksheet in stacked format

Step 4 – Analyse experimental results

- Session window output (Analysis of variance table)
- Factorial Plots (main effects, interaction effects)
- Residual plots (residuals versus fits, residuals versus order, probability plot of residuals)

Step 5 – Summarise and validate results

- Identify significant effects
- Confirm validity of model

17.02 Two Way ANOVA (Balanced ANOVA)

Used for testing for differences between the means of the levels for each of two different factors. (Eg; a final product is produced using different raw material suppliers and different processing temperatures. A result (such as final strength) achieved with different suppliers and temperatures can be tested for differences in means for each of the two different factors.)

Assumptions:

- Constant Error Variance: Residuals versus Fits show no patterns
- Normality of Error: Residuals are approximately normal
- Independence of Error: Residuals versus Order of Data show no patterns
- If measurements are not repeated – no interactions between row and column factors (interactions can be determined with replicated values)

The Null and Alternative Hypothesis for the row & column factors are:

ROW FACTOR

H_0: The means of row factors are all equal

H_A: Not all means of row factors are equal

COLUMN FACTOR

H_0: The means of column factors are all equal

H_A: Not all means of column factors are equal

The test:

1. Choose **Stat > ANOVA > Balanced ANOVA**

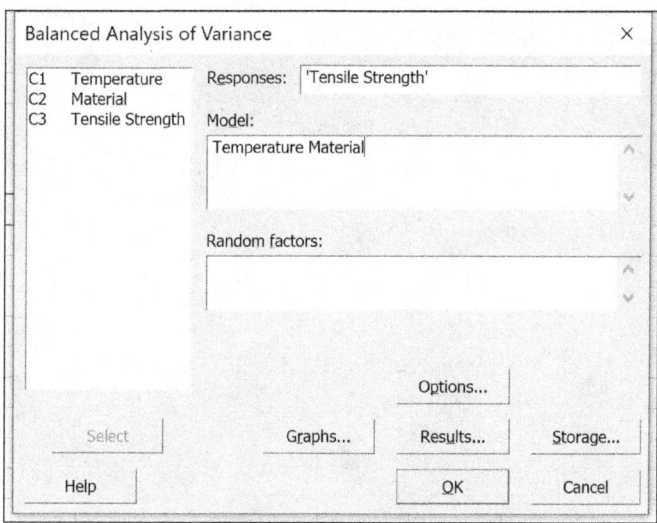

2. **Responses:** (insert column containing the response variable)
3. **Model:** (insert columns containing the categorical variables being studied)
4. Select **Graphs**

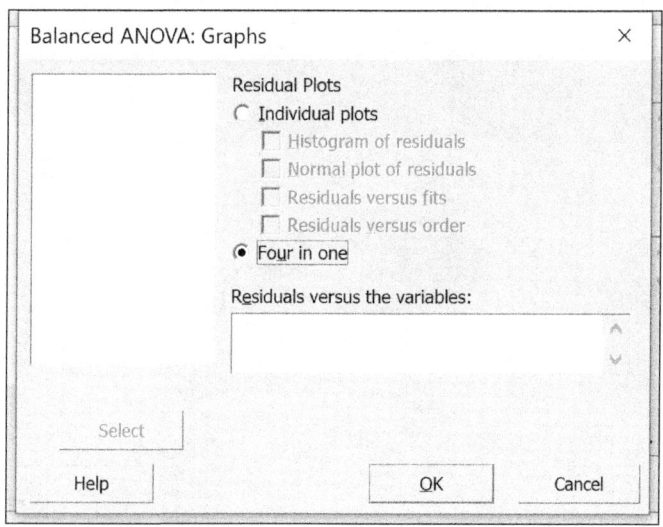

5. **Residual Plots:** check **Four in one**
6. Click **OK** in all dialogue boxes

NOTE: Data must be stacked for Minitab analysis, cannot analyse data in a matrix format.

Factor Information

Factor	Type	Levels	Values
Temperature	Fixed	2	high, low
Material	Fixed	2	A, B

Analysis of Variance for Tensile Strength

Source	DF	SS	MS	F	P
Temperature	1	59.29	59.29	3.91	0.069
Material	1	915.06	915.06	60.41	0.000
Error	13	196.93	15.15		
Total	15	1171.28			

Model Summary

S	R-sq	R-sq(adj)
3.89208	83.19%	80.60%

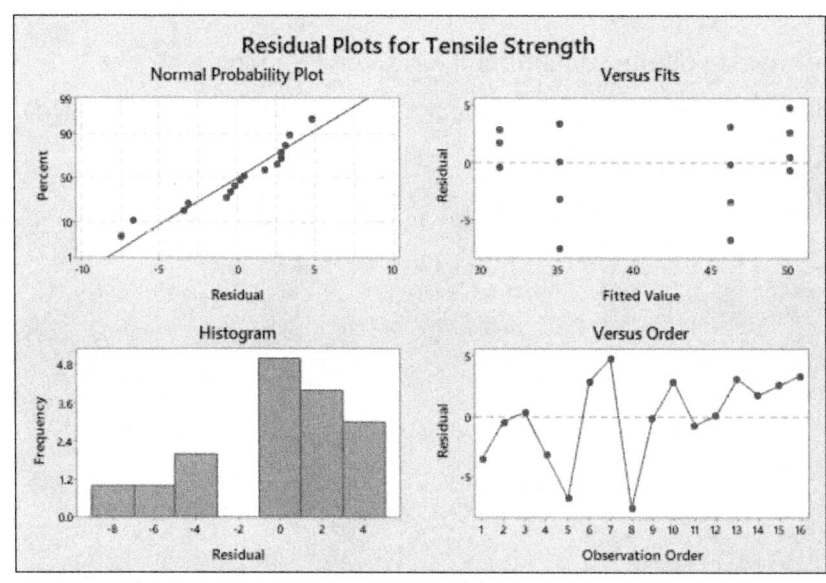

17.03 Main Effects Plot

1. Choose **Stat > ANOVA > Main Effects Plot**

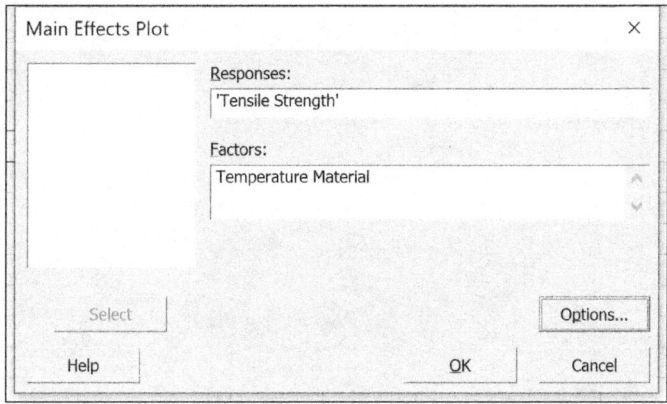

2. **Responses:** (insert column containing the response or independent variable)
3. **Factors:** (insert columns containing factor or dependent variables)
4. Click **OK**

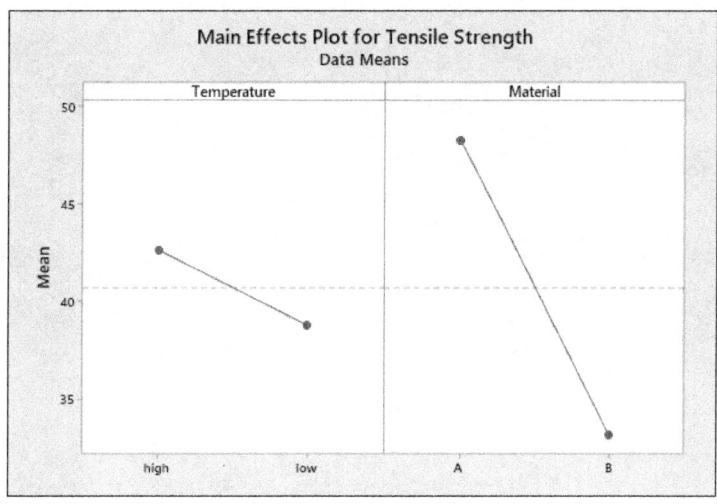

17.04 Interactions Plot

1. Choose **Stat > ANOVA > Interactions Plot**

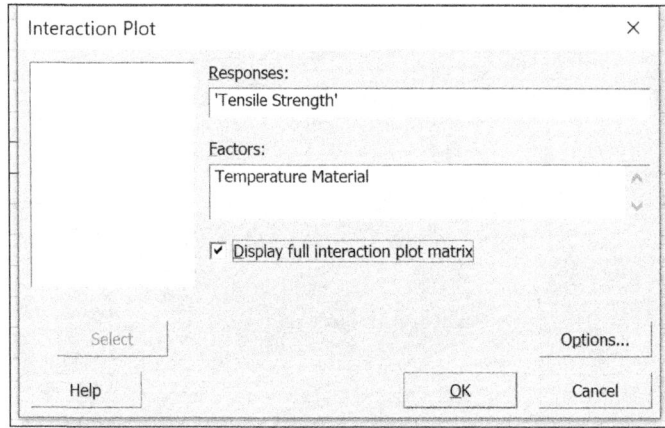

2. **Responses:** (insert column containing the response or independent variable)
3. **Factors:** (insert columns containing factor or dependent variables)
4. **Display full interaction plot matrix:** (check)
5. Click **OK**

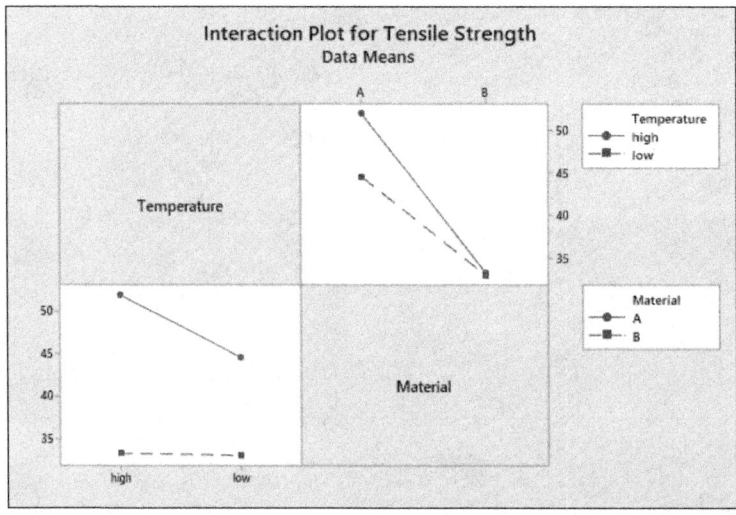

18. DESIGN OF EXPERIMENTS (FACTORIAL)

A systematic approach that minimises the number of trials run to perform an experiment to determine what major input and process X's impacts the output Y.

TYPE OF DESIGN	PRACTICAL NUMBER OF X's	USED WHEN WANT TO IDENTIFY -
SCREENING (Resolution III)	Greater than 5	Main Effects
FRACTIONAL FACTORIALS	3 to 10	Main effects and some interactions
FULL FACTORIALS	2 to 5	All main effects and interactions

18.01 Experimental Design Process

An experiment is designed and conducted according to the following process.

Step 1 – Identify responses, factors and factor levels

- Low and high level settings
- Center points

Step 2 – Select type of design

- Full factorial (Full Resolution)
- Fractional factorial (Resolution IV and V)
- Screening design (Resolution III)

Step 3 – Check Orthogonality of the design

Step 4 – Run experiment

- Run in the randomised order shown on the worksheet
- Insert data directly into worksheet

Step 5 – Analyse experimental results

- Session window output (effects, aliasing)
- Effects Plots
- Factorial Plots (main effects, interaction effects, cube plots)

Step 6 – Reduce the model

- Drop insignificant terms

Step 7 – Validate and summarise the results

- Identify significant effects
- Confirm validity of model
- Residual plots (residuals versus fits, residuals versus order, probability plot of residuals)

18.02 Check Orthogonality of the Design

If columns of a design are orthogonal:
- The sum of each column = zero
- The correlation between columns = zero

With an orthogonal design:
- Terms are estimated independently
- Effects are independent of each other – all insignificant terms can be removed simultaneously (reduced model)

18.03 Designing the Experiment

This design will provide you with all the information needed to determine main effects and interactions of a number of factors.

Designing the Experiment:

1. Choose **Stat > DOE > Factorial > Create Factorial Design**

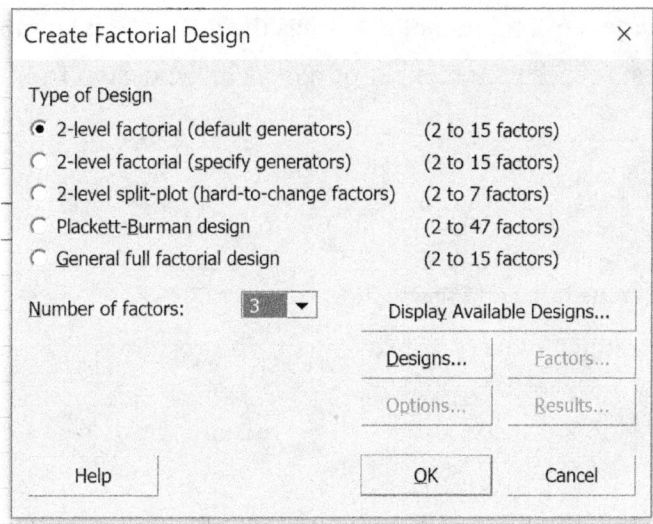

2. **Type of Design:** (choose type of design)
3. **Number of factors:** (select number of factors)
4. Select **Designs**

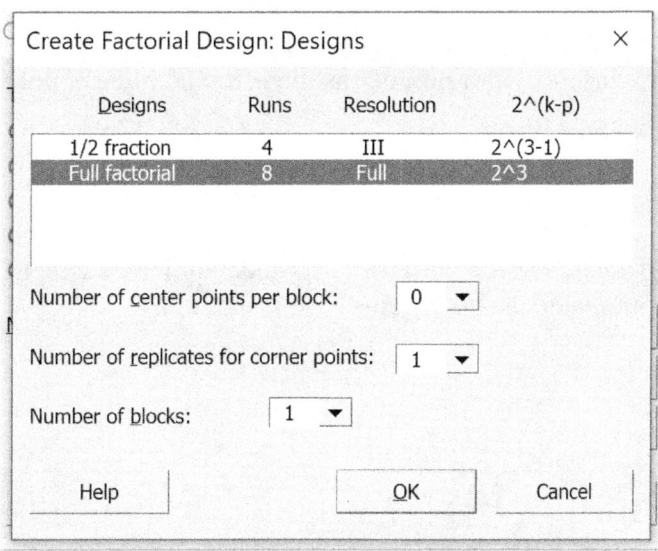

5. **Designs:** (choose <u>full</u> factorial or <u>fractional</u> factorial design)
6. **Number of center points:** (select number of center points to be added per block – when working with both text and numeric factors there is no true center to the design)

7. **Number of replicates:** (select number of times the design will be run or replicated)
8. **Number of blocks:** (choose the number of blocks in the design from the available numbers)
9. Click **OK**
10. Select **Factors**

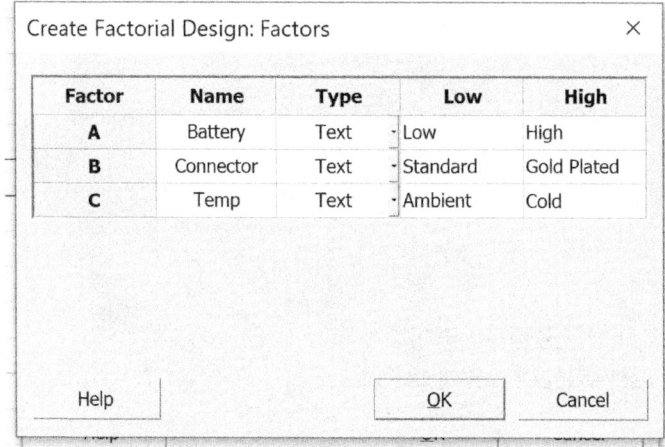

11. **Name:** (insert name of factors), **Type:** (select numeric or text), **Low and High:** (insert values, for numeric insert lowest number as the low, and highest number as the high)
12. Click **OK** in all dialogue boxes

Note About Error Terms:

Residuals (error terms) are generated with center points, replicated experiments, and in some reduced models. Without residuals, no P-values are generated.

18.04 Analysing the Experiment

1. Choose **Stat > DOE > Factorial > Analyse Factorial Design**

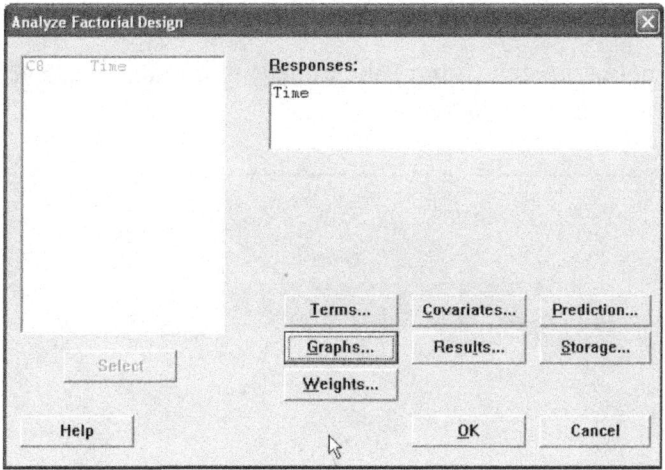

2. **Response:** (insert column containing the response variable)
3. Select **Graphs**

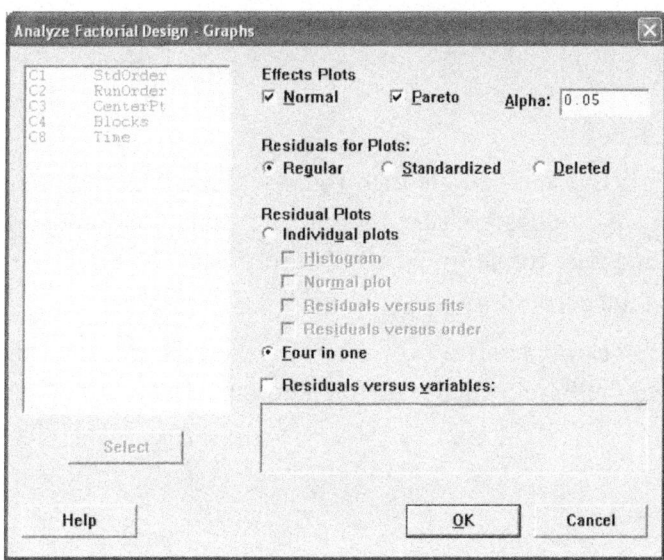

4. **Effects plots:** (check **Pareto** and **Normal**)

5. Click **OK** in all dialogue boxes

Pareto Chart of Effects

The Pareto Chart of Effects shows the magnitude of the effect, not the direction of the effect.

When error terms are not estimated (non-replication), significance tests are based on Psuedo Standard Error (PSE) using Lenth's Method.

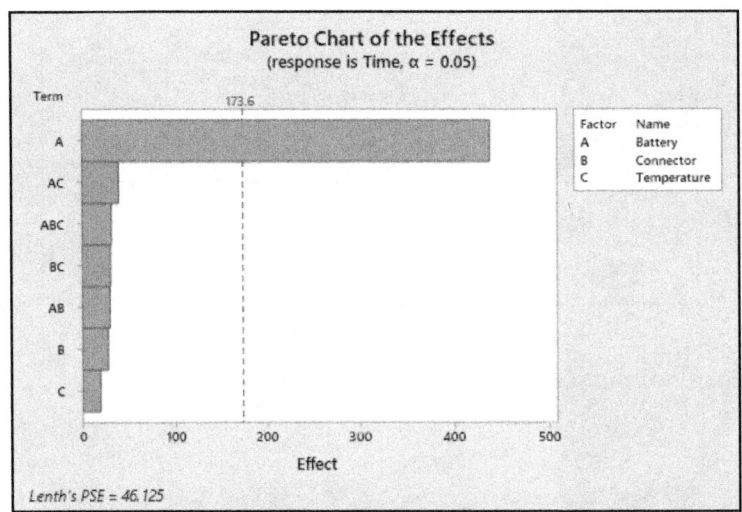

P-Values

(P-Values) Where the p-value for a single factor is = < alpha, that factor significantly impacts the response Y. Where a p-value is > alpha, then the term may be removed from the analysis and the equation (reduced models) for simplification purposes as it's effect on the response Y is not significantly different than zero.

When error terms are not estimated (non-replication - see image below) then p-values will not be visible so we refer to the Pareto Chart of effects to guide us in reducing the model.

Coded Coefficients

Term	Effect	Coef	SE Coef	T-Value	P-Value	VIF
Constant		302.3	*	*	*	
Battery	437.5	218.8	*	*	*	1.00
Connector	-28.50	-14.25	*	*	*	1.00
Temperature	20.00	10.00	*	*	*	1.00
Battery*Connector	-30.50	-15.25	*	*	*	1.00
Battery*Temperature	40.00	20.00	*	*	*	1.00
Connector*Temperature	-31.00	-15.50	*	*	*	1.00
Battery*Connector*Temperature	-32.00	-16.00	*	*	*	1.00

Model Summary

S	R-sq	R-sq(adj)	R-sq(pred)
*	100.00%	*	*

Screening Design

Screening designs are used to determine at a high level, the direction for improvement and what are the most significant factors from a large list of factors. A screening design is useful when you have a limited budget and cannot afford to perform a full factorial experiment. Usually **resolution III** designs – main effects and second order and higher interactions are confounded.

18.05 Reducing the Model

Used after the initial analysis (full and fractional factorial experiments) for dropping terms from the experiment model (equation) that do not have any significance.

When error terms are not estimated (non-replication), significance tests are based on Psuedo Standard Error (PSE) using Lenth's Method. With this in mind, the most effective process for dropping terms is:

    Step 1: Remove insignificant terms of the highest order and analyse

    Step 2: Remove insignificant terms of the next highest order and analyse

    Step 3: Continue with step 2 until ending with main effects

NOTE: When an interaction term is included in the model, the parent factor must be left in the model.

Dropping terms and analysing the experiment:

1. Choose **Stat > DOE > Factorial > Analyse Factorial Design**
2. **Response:** (insert column containing the response variable)
3. Select **Terms**

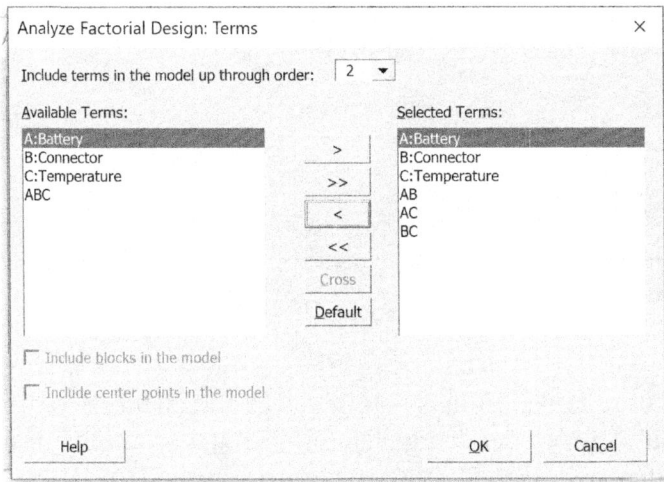

4. Drop terms from the list of 'selected terms' by selecting and clicking on the arrows
5. Click **OK**
6. Select **Graphs**
7. **Effects plots:** (check pareto)
8. **Residual plots:** (check 'four in one' when analysing your final model)
9. Click **OK** in all dialogue boxes

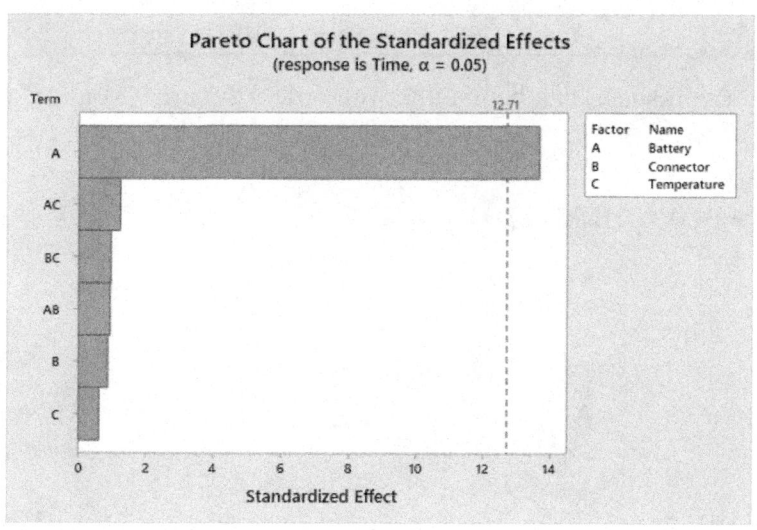

Coded Coefficients

Term	Effect	Coef	SE Coef	T-Value	P-Value	VIF
Constant		302.3	16.0	18.89	0.034	
Battery	437.5	218.8	16.0	13.67	0.046	1.00
Connector	-28.5	-14.3	16.0	-0.89	0.537	1.00
Temperature	20.0	10.0	16.0	0.63	0.644	1.00
Battery*Connector	-30.5	-15.3	16.0	-0.95	0.515	1.00
Battery*Temperature	40.0	20.0	16.0	1.25	0.430	1.00
Connector*Temperature	-31.0	-15.5	16.0	-0.97	0.510	1.00

Model Summary

S	R-sq	R-sq(adj)	R-sq(pred)
45.2548	99.48%	96.36%	66.76%

Notice that when you reduce the model, p-values are now calculated.

18.06 Changing The Way The Design Is Displayed

The design display (worksheet) can be in either run order (the order you use to run the experiment) or in standard order. It can also be displayed in uncoded units (as input by the user) or coded units (1, -1).

1. Choose **Stat > DOE > Display Design**

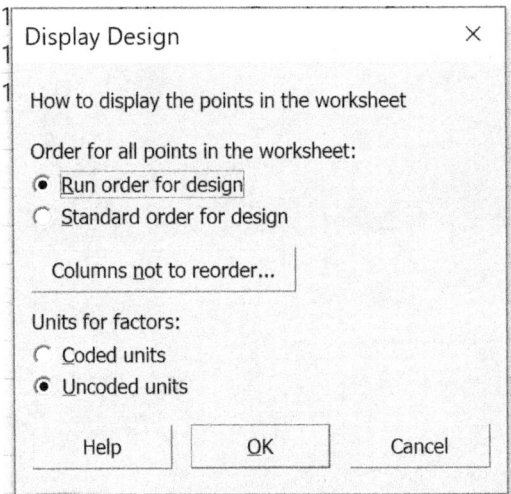

2. **Order for all points in the worksheet:** (check run order or standard order)
3. **Units for factors:** (check coded or uncoded)
4. Click **OK**

18.07 Check Validity of the Model Using Residuals

The validity of the model produced by any factorial design is determined by a study of residuals. The assumptions associated with the model are:

Normality of Error:

Errors should be normally distributed with a mean of zero - NORMAL PROBABILITY PLOT – should be close to a straight line.

Constant Error Variance:

The error variance does not change for different levels of a factor or according to the values of the predicted response - RESIDUALS VERSUS THE FITTED VALUES PLOT – variation remains constant for all fitted values.

Independence of Errors:

Each error (residual) is independent of all other errors - RESIDUALS VERSUS THE ORDER OF THE DATA – no obvious patterns indicating a time related effect.

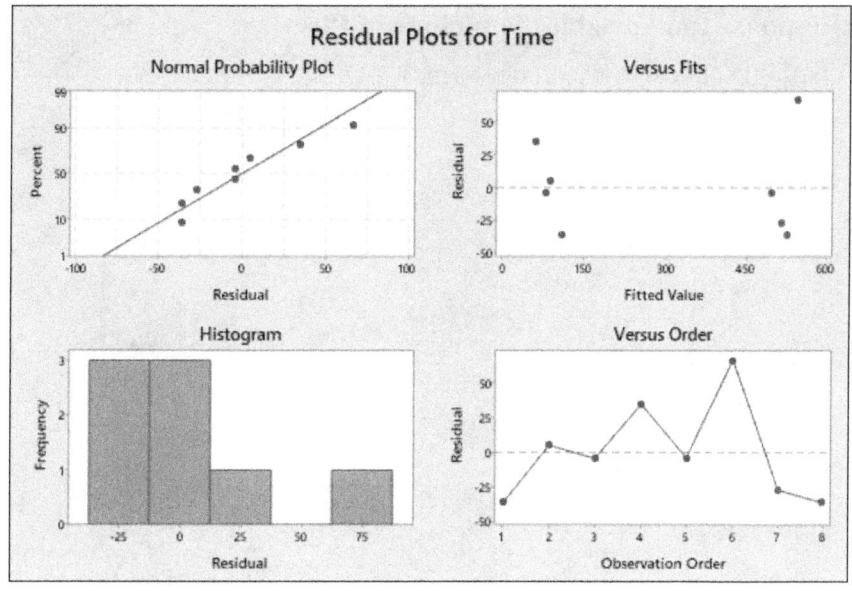

18.08 Factorial Plots for Designed Experiments

1. Choose **Stat > DOE > Factorial > Factorial Plots**

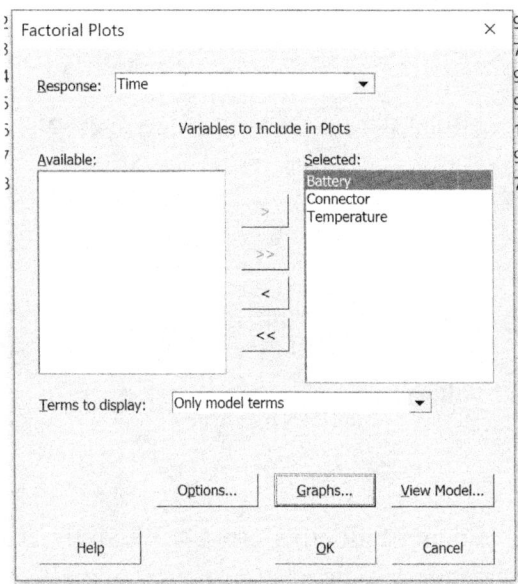

2. Select the **Response** and **Variables to Include in Plots**
3. **Terms to display:** (choose only model terms)
4. Select **Graphs**

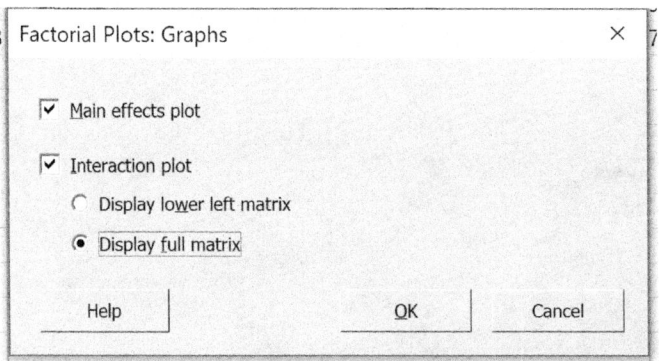

5. Check **Main effects plot**
6. Check **Interaction plot**

7. Check **Display full matrix**
8. Click **OK**

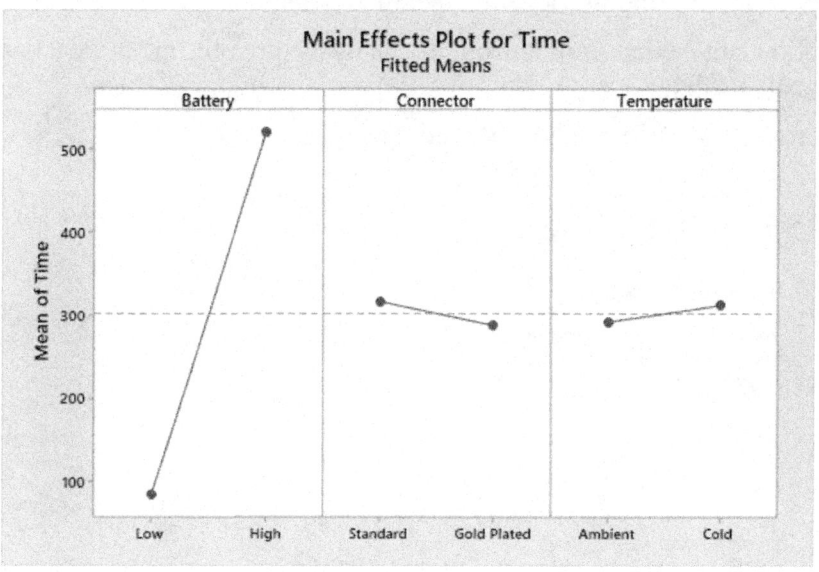

18.09 Response Optimization

Response optimisation is used to identify the combination of input variable settings that jointly optimise a specific single response or set of specific responses.

An optimal solution can be determined from the analysis of experiment data so you need to complete your analysis first.

1. Choose **Stat > DOE > Factorial > Response Optimiser**

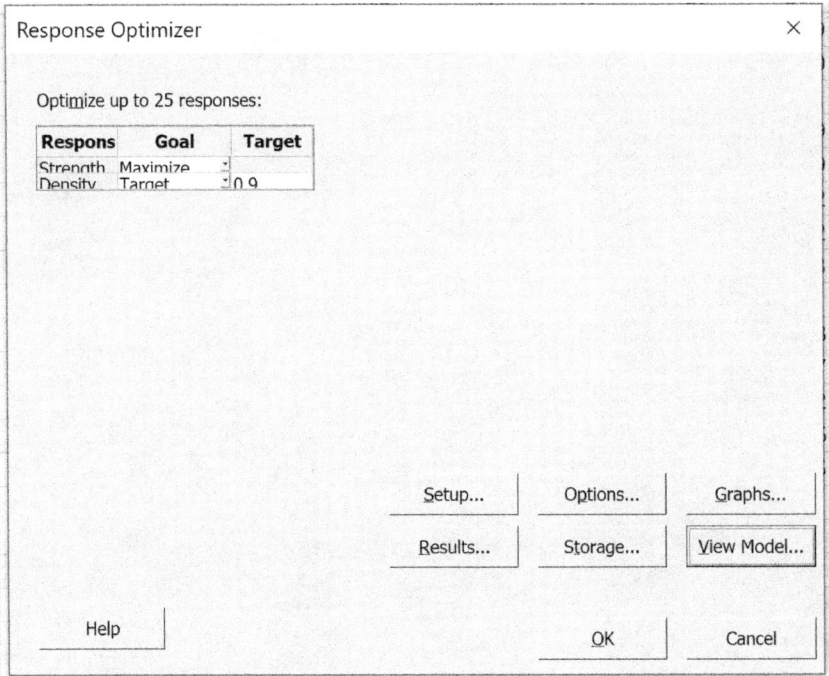

2. In the table under **Goal**, select one of the following options for each response:
    a. **Do not optimize:** Do not include the response in the optimization process.
    b. **Minimize:** Lower values of the response are preferable.
    c. **Target:** The response is optimal when values meet a specific target value.
    d. **Maximize:** Higher values of the response are preferable.
3. Select **Setup**

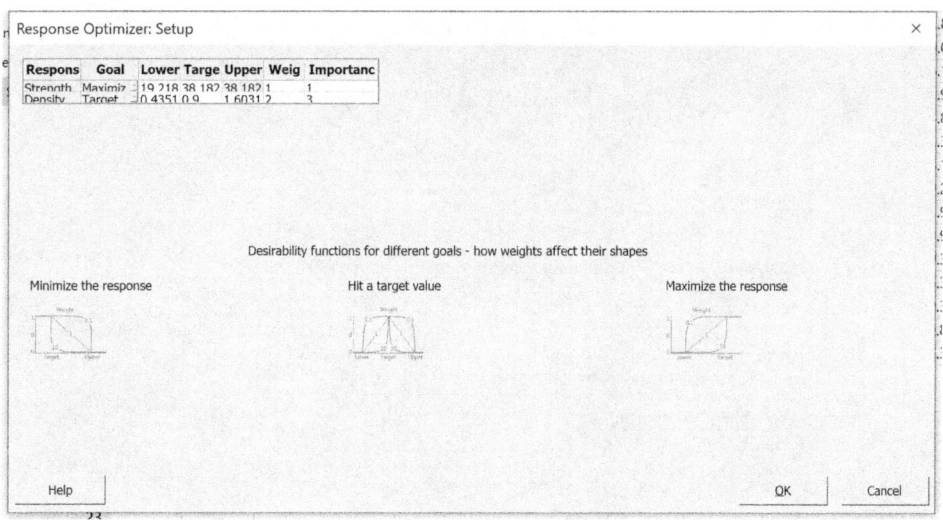

a. **Response** - displays all the responses that are included in the optimization. This column does not take any input.

b. **Goal** - displays the goal that you specified for each response. This column does not take any input.

c. **Lower** - for each response that has a goal of Target or Maximize, enter a lower boundary. By default, Minitab uses the minimum value in the data.

d. **Target** - enter a target value for each response. If your goal is to target a specific value, the target value is the target that you entered in the main dialog box. If your goal is to minimize the response, by default, Minitab sets the target value at the minimum value of the data. If your goal is to maximize the response, Minitab sets the target value to the maximum value of the data.

e. **Upper** - for each response that has a goal of Minimize or Target, enter an upper boundary. By default, Minitab uses the maximum value in the data.

f. **Weight** - enter a number from 0.1 to 10 to define the shape for the desirability function.

g. **Importance** - enter a number from 0.1 to 10 to specify the comparative importance of the response.

4. **Repeat for each response variable** included in the optimization
5. Click **OK**

Parameters

Response	Goal	Lower	Target	Upper	Weight	Importance
Time	Maximum	72	612		1	1

Solution

Solution	Battery	Connector	Temperature	Time Fit	Composite Desirability
1	High	Standard	Cold	545.25	0.876389

Multiple Response Prediction

Variable	Setting
Battery	High
Connector	Standard
Temperature	Cold

Response	Fit	SE Fit	95% CI	95% PI
Time	545.3	33.6	(452.0, 638.5)	(383.7, 706.8)

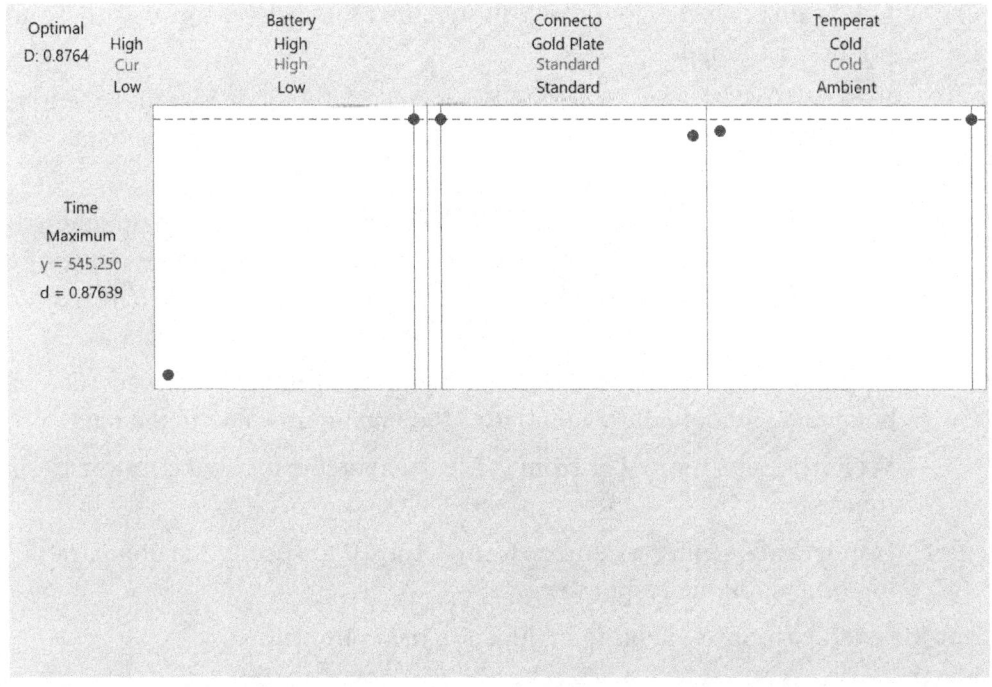

19. BIBLIOGRAPHY

Lee Sye, G.W., (2004), *'Process Mastery with Lean Six Sigma 2nd Edition: A Guide to the Application of Six Sigma for Process Improvement Project Team Leaders'*, Soarent, Australia.
ISBN: 9780645718201

Hoerl, R., Snee, R.D., (2002), *'Statistical Thinking"*, Duxbury, Pacific Grove.
ISBN: 0-534-38158-8

Levine, D.M., Ramsey, P.P., Smidt, R.K., (2001), *'Applied Statistics for Engineers and Scientists'*, Prentice Hall, NewJersey.
ISBN: 0-13-488801-4

20. THE AUTHOR

George Lee Sye was born in 1959, he has found his niche as an author, influence and persuasion educator, and business improvement trainer and coach.

George founded Soarent Vision Pty Ltd in 2000 and has continually run that company as Managing Director.

He founded his first Professional Learning Hub in 2016, and then converted this into what is now the 9 Skills Factory professional development platform. He is the site's lead trainer and this is where he delivers the bulk of his business improvement and leadership education to the world.

More information can be found at - www.9skillsfactory.com

George's fascination with human behaviour started in the mid 1980s. Intent on understanding how to accelerate the process of building connection and rapport with people in his work, he began a journey of discovery that has now influenced every aspect of his life, both personal and professional.

Through his seminars, personal coaching, audio and printed books, George has devoted himself to passing on his knowledge and skill for creating a remarkable quality of life. What he has learnt through reading, trial and error and an incredible diversity of experiences is now the foundation for positively impacting the lives of literally thousands of people.

George's goal has always been to communicate to people in simple and practical terms using life examples that people can relate to. His success in this area has come predominantly through his belief that delivering an idea without a way of using it is nothing more than giving people another topic of conversation. Unless the idea converts to some form of action or behavioural change that positively affects a person's life, it is a waste of time.

His ability to simplify what are often considered to be complex topics is remarkable. As a result, he has been able to create considerable value for companies with whom he has worked in the area of business improvement, and his popularity as a corporate educator, speaker and personal coach has grown consistently.

George launched his podcast The George Experiment in 2018.

Photo of the author riding at Phillip Island GP Circuit is courtesy of SD Pics Photography

George is also an avid motorcycle enthusiast with the ultimate part time job as an on track ride coach with the California Superbike School.

Since 2002 he has written a multitude of books, most of which are now distributed on Amazon and on iTunes in digital form. For more information about George and his work, visit his web sites.

georgeleesye.com / 9skillsfactory.com
---------- END ----------

Printed in Dunstable, United Kingdom